CROWS,
PAPUA NEW GUINEA,
AND BOATS

30127085130602

Copyright © David Thorne 2018 All rights reserved.

ISBN 978-0-9886895-4-1
Crows, Papua New Guinea, and Boats
A new collection of irreverence

david@27bslash6.com

This book is sold subject to the condition that it shall not, by way of trade or otherwise, be lent, re-sold, hired out, re-produced on the internet or otherwise circulated without the author's prior consent in any form of binding or cover other than that in which it is published and without a similar condition including this condition being imposed on the subsequent purchaser. Activities and vehicle modifications appearing or described in this book may be potentially dangerous.

Also available by the same author:

The Internet is a Playground
Making its debut at #4 on The New York Times Best Seller list, *The Internet is a Playground* includes articles from 27bslash6 plus over 160 pages of new material.

I'll Go Home Then; It's Warm and Has Chairs
Featuring new articles from 27bslash6 along with previously unpublished material.

The Collected Works of 27b/6 - Victorian Edition
Illustrated and abridged for polite society.

Look Evelyn, Duck Dynasty Wiper Blades, We Should Get Them
A collection of new essays.

That's Not How You Wash a Squirrel
A collection of new essays and emails.

Wrap It In a Bit of Cheese Like You're Tricking the Dog
The fifth collection of new essays and emails.

Walk It Off, Princess

For Holly and Seb. Airways.

Special shout-out to my neighbor's retarded dogs, Dawkins and Sully, whose incessant barking and weird-arse howling has kept me constant company. Honestly, it sounds like a ninety-year-old man with throat cancer yodeling while his wife yells, "Jack!"

Reviews

★★★★☆ "There were no instructions but it wasn't difficult to work out. Just make sure you have a friend and a size 11 spanner handy."
Beverly Gardner

★★★★★ "Bought this as a gift for my dad as he lost his hat. He loves it and has received many compliments from elderly women."
Andrew Snell

★★★★★ "It smells terrible but achieved good results with very little scrubbing. My advice is to spray it and run away as quickly as you can."
Richard Morris

★☆☆☆☆ "Not waterproof. I tested it in a bucket of water and it lasted less than ten minutes."
Dave Pease

★★★★☆ "Pros: Took this bad boy camping last week and all of my camp buddies were jealous. Cons: There isn't any way of attaching it to your leg. I tried using Velcro but it fell off when I jumped out of a tree."
Korneel Bullens

Contents

Crows 23

Papua New Guinea 91

Boats 139

Introduction

So you've heard the Siren's song: irresistible, tantalizing, filling your head with visions of being wrapped in warm, gentle winds as you travel across calm seas, experiencing sunrises that take your breath away and relaxing in quiet coves. In other words, you want to buy a boat.

What attracts you to the idea of boating? Is it speeding through the water with grandma in a tube? Is it fishing for hours in the middle of a lake or heading out for an overnight cruise to other ports?

Crows, Papua New Guinea, and Boats takes you through the process of deciding whether boating is for you and provides a comprehensive guide to everything you need to know about owning, operating, and maintaining a boat. For those with some boating experience but haven't yet bought a boat, this book escorts you through the process. If you already have a boat but want to know more about how to pilot it, equip it, store it, tow it, or handle emergencies on it, this is the book for you. Even if you already have experience captaining your own boat, this book will help fill in some gaps in your knowledge and provide tips for improving your boating experience. As we say in the boating world, *bow thrusters to eight!*

Foreword

From: David Thorne
Date: Monday 8 October 2018 10.15am
To: Ricky Gervais
Subject: Foreword

Dear Ricky,

Hope you are doing well. Big fan of your earlier work.

You may not remember, but you followed me on Twitter for two weeks then unfollowed me after writing an article for the *Huffington Post* and calling it *The Internet is My Playground*. It was a bit of a dick move but these things happen. It's been 5 years, 3 months and 27 days since you unfollowed me and I'm not one to carry a grudge.

As you owe me, I was wondering if you'd write the foreword for my book. I don't have a title yet and have only completed 16 pages but it's mostly about crows, Papua New Guinea, and boats so far.

My deadline to have the book completed (including copy, cover, layout and foreword), is next Wednesday so if you could have something to me by the end of the week, that would be perfect.

Regards, David Thorne

From: Ricky Gervais
Date: Wednesday 10 October 2018 2.06pm
To: David Thorne
Subject: Re: Foreword

Right name wrong person.
I'm Canadian. Ricky Gervais the comedian is British.

How did you get this email address?

From: David Thorne
Date: Wednesday 10 October 2018 2.28pm
To: Ricky Gervais
Subject: Re: Re: Foreword

Hello Ricky,

Thank you for getting back to me so quickly. .

Your email address is on the contact page of your website. I thought it slightly odd that a multi-award winning comedian would be running a vinyl cutting business from his garage but who am I to judge?

Have you considered going by Rick to avoid this type of confusion?

Regards, David

From: Ricky Gervais
Date: Wednesday 10 October 2018 4.11pm
To: David Thorne
Subject: Re: Re: Re: Foreword

Why should I? Tell the comedian to change his name. And it's not a garage. What's your problem?

From: David Thorne
Date: Wednesday 10 October 2018 4.20pm
To: Ricky Gervais
Subject: Re: Re: Re: Re: Foreword

Ricky,

I don't have a problem. You're the one pretending to be Ricky Gervais.

Regards, David

From: Ricky Gervais
Date: Wednesday 10 October 2018 4.34pm
To: David Thorne
Subject: Re: Re: Re: Re: Re: Foreword

I'm not pretending to be anyone asshole. You emailed me.

From: David Thorne
Date: Wednesday 10 October 2018 4.49pm
To: Ricky Gervais
Subject: Re: Re: Re: Re: Re: Re: Foreword

Ricky,

Only due to false representation. There's no disclaimer or even an asterisk on your website to alert visitors to the fact that you're not a British comedian. One might easily be forgiven for interpreting the sparkling Comic-Sans typeface and rotating mailbox gif as parody.

Regardless, how are you going with the foreword?

Regards, David

From: Ricky Gervais
Date: Wednesday 10 October 2018 5.16pm
To: David Thorne
Subject: Re: Re: Re: Re: Re: Re: Re: Foreword

I'm not writing the foreword.

And who asked for your opinion? Stay the fuck off my website if you don't like it.

I'm adding your email address to my spam filter.

....

From: David Thorne
Date: Wednesday 10 October 2018 5.23pm
To: Ricky Gervais
Subject: Re: Re: Re: Re: Re: Re: Re: Re: Foreword

Ricky,

How will I contact you if I need vinyl-cut registration numbers for a boat? Do you have a telephone number I can reach you on?

Regards, David

From: Ricky Gervais
Date: Thursday 11 October 2018 9.38am
To: David Thorne
Subject: Re: Re: Re: Re: Re: Re: Re: Re: Foreword

Do you need registration numbers for a boat?

From: David Thorne
Date: Thursday 11 October 2018 10.04am
To: Ricky Gervais
Subject: Re: Re: Re: Re: Re: Re: Re: Re: Re: Foreword

No. Just the foreword.

From: Ricky Gervais
Date: Thursday 11 October 2018 10.15am
To: David Thorne
Subject: Re: Re: Re: Re: Re: Re: Re: Re: Re: Re: Foreword

Well fuck off then.

From: David Thorne
Date: Thursday 11 October 2018 10.22am
To: Ricky Gervais
Subject: Re: Re: Re: Re: Re: Re: Re: Re: Re: Re: Re: Foreword

Ricky,

Can I at least get a quote?

Regards, David

From: Ricky Gervais
Date: Thursday 11 October 2018 10.41am
To: David Thorne
Subject: Re: Re: Re: Re: Re: Re: Re: Re: Re: Re: Re: Re: Foreword

For vinyl registration numbers?

From: David Thorne
Date: Thursday 11 October 2018 10.56am
To: Ricky Gervais
Subject: Re: Re: Re: Re: Re: Re: Re: Re: Re: Re: Re: Re: Re: Foreword

No, for the front cover of my book.

Something along the lines of "Best book about crows, Papua New Guinea, and boats I've ever read" will do. I wouldn't spend too much time on it, you probably have a ton of telephone numbers for the back of vans to cut out.

Regards, David

....

From: Ricky Gervais
Date: Thursday 11 October 2018 1.31pm
To: David Thorne
Subject: Re: Re: Re: Re: Re: Re: Re: Re: Re: Re: Re: Re: Re: Re: Foreword

Here's a quote for you: Fuck off. You can't just get a quote from someone and say it's from someone else. That's fraud. And FYI we do banners, wall graphics, yard signs, flags, tents and signage. Not just vehicle decals asshole. Grow the fuck up.

From: David Thorne
Date: Thursday 11 October 2018 1.40pm
To: Ricky Gervais
Subject: Re: Re: Re: Re: Re: Re: Re: Re: Re: Re: Re: Re: Re: Re: Re: Re: Foreword

It's a bit wordy but I appreciate the effort. I'll probably just go with the one about it being the best book about crows, Papua New Guinea, and boats you've ever read.

Regards, David

....

From: Ricky Gervais
Date: Thursday 11 October 2018 1.57pm
To: David Thorne
Subject: Re: Re: Re: Re: Re: Re: Re: Re: Re: Re: Re: Re: Re: Re: Re: Re: Re: Foreword

I didn't say that, you did.

From: David Thorne
Date: Thursday 11 October 2018 2.13pm
To: Ricky Gervais
Subject: Re: Re: Re: Re: Re: Re: Re: Re: Re: Re: Re: Re: Re: Re: Re: Re Foreword

Say what?

From: Ricky Gervais
Date: Thursday 11 October 2018 3.14pm
To: David Thorne
Subject: Re: Re: Re: Re: Re: Re: Re: Re: Re: Re: Re: Re: Re: Re: Re: Re: Re Foreword

Like I'd fall for that. Are you 12?

From: David Thorne
Date: Thursday 11 October 2018 3.21pm
To: Ricky Gervais
Subject: Re: Re: Re: Re: Re: Re: Re: Re: Re: Re: Re: Re: Re: Re: Re: Re: Re: Re Foreword

Please, I'm not the one pretending to be someone else online. There's a term for people like you. Catburgler.

From: Ricky Gervais
Date: Thursday 11 October 2018 4.04pm
To: David Thorne
Subject: Re: Re: Re: Re: Re: Re: Re: Re: Re: Re: Re: Re: Re: Re: Re: Re: Re: Re: Re: Foreword

Fuck you. You're the catburgler.

Scratch 'n Sniff

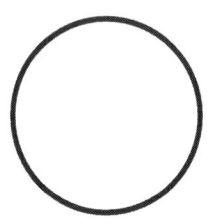

◯

Crows

It's been said that revenge harms those seeking it more than those it's directed at but nobody believes this. It's the kind of thing people who think they are better than everyone else like to say. The type of people who smirk and shake their heads and make a little 'hff' noise with their nose when you admit that you don't only buy organic free-range eggs from farms that play Dave Matthews to the chickens and deliver their produce by solar powered land yachts built from kelp.

"Have you seen the movie *John Wick*?"
"Hff. No, I only watch subtitled Cambodian movies about transsexual rice farmers. Have you seen *Hgheú Oân Tchâio*? It's pretty much my favorite movie by acclaimed director Chói Hzgú."
"No."
"Hff. You should. He films everything on a 1967 Honeywell Elmo Super Filmatic 104 camera upside-down through cheesecloth in the rain. His first film, *Ngângut*, is forty-six hours long.
"I like movies with robots in them."
"Hff. Of course you do. Well, if you'll excuse me, I have a gluten protest to attend. We're going to dress up as loaves of bread and block traffic."

John Wick would have been ten minutes long if the lead character shrugged his shoulders and said, "They killed my puppy but the best revenge is moving on and getting over it so I'll just listen to my new Hang Drum CD in the bath and get an early night."

We're hard-wired for revenge. Be it leveling the homes of religious fanatics who fly planes into buildings or urinating in Peter Jackson's backpack for telling classmates not to play handball with you because you have 'the anus AIDS', revenge is a part of the genetic makeup we share with every other animal. Apes will throw a mother's baby out of a tree over stolen fruit, octopuses will break off a sharp piece of coral and shank other octopuses for having brighter colors, and wasps will fuck you up for glancing at them. Once, while camping, my offspring Seb and I were trapped inside a tent for two hours after he glanced at a wasp. It was probably more like thirty minutes but it felt like two hours because there was nothing to do. We played I-Spy for a while but after tent, zipper, screen and wasp were used, we just sat quietly. The only animals more vengeful than wasps are crows.

A lot has been documented about the intelligence of crows. They're far more intelligent than dolphins or monkeys and are capable of solving complex problems that stump many humans. I read about a test once where they placed a crow in a room with a dismantled engine block from a 2006 Toyota Camry and it built a robot exoskeleton and escaped by blasting through a concrete wall.

I had a pet crow for an hour once. I named him Flash because my class had recently taken a school excursion to the local cinema to see *Flash Gordon*. Our teacher, Mr Mercury, was a huge fan of the band Queen and, sharing the last name of the group's lead singer, loved it when people asked if he was related to Freddie. He said he was, and that Freddie had been to his house several times, but I've learnt since that Freddie Mercury's real name was Farrokh Bulsara so I call bullshit. Mr Mercury also told us that he could hold his breath underwater for three minutes but who can trust anything he claimed? I saw him at a basketball game years later and I thought about saying something but he was a couple of seats down and several across and he'd lost a hand somehow. He had one of those beige attachments with a stainless steel claw and pulleys.*

At the time, I felt *Flash Gordon* was pretty much the greatest cinematic masterpiece ever created. I've seen it since and it's not. The soundtrack is okay but special-

---

* *I know a guy named Jeff who also has a claw hand. I asked him if it gives him an advantage when he plays the claw machines at arcades and he replied, "I've never played one. But probably." My friend Ross is excellent at them but he doesn't have a claw hand, he's just semi-autistic and practices at home with a Lego Technic crane.*

effects-wise, it's hard to believe it was filmed two years after *Star Wars*. You'd think someone in production would have asked, "Who signed off on this? I can see the strings on the hawk men. Has anyone here seen *Star Wars*? It's a lot better than this."

I returned home from school one afternoon to discover our dog, Gus, barking and clawing frenziedly at a glass fireplace screen in our living room. A crow had somehow found its way down the chimney and couldn't get back up past the flue. I've no idea how long it had flapped about, desperately attempting to escape, but it was huddled in a corner when I found it, exhausted and seemingly accepting of its fate.* I used a pair of oven mitts to lift the crow out of the fireplace, wary of its sharp beak, but it made no attempt to peck me.

Our front yard contained a single large maple that shaded the driveway. It was tall enough to climb and had once featured a tire-swing until the rope snapped and my sister was hospitalized with a collapsed lung. It wasn't the fall

---

* *I experience the same thing whenever my partner Holly and I argue. Just last night, she went off because I threw out a Tupperware bowl. It didn't matter that the lid had been missing for two years, it was her favorite Tupperware bowl and she loved it more than she has ever loved anything in her life. Apparently I only throw out her stuff, not mine, but that's because my stuff isn't garbage.*

that caused the injury, it was that she was sitting inside the tire when the rope broke, mid-swing, and bounced out of the front yard into traffic. My father accused me of pushing the swing too hard but really, if you are going to build a swing for your kids, use decent rope - not four pieces of polyester line from a Coleman tent tied together.

I placed the crow gently on the grass under the maple, stroking its glossy blue-black back with a now gloveless hand and talking it through the ordeal. It was too long ago to recall exactly what was said but it was probably along the lines of, "It'll be alright. Sorry about the dog. I'm going to name you Flash."

My family had pets with worse names - Gus was short for Asparagus and we once had a cat named Heather Locklear Ballerina Disney. My sister was told she could name the cat but that doesn't mean agreeing to the first thing that pops out of her mouth. Whenever anybody asked me what the cat's name was, I told them it was Buck Rogers, which is a much better name. Heather Locklear Ballerina Disney eventually hung herself on a Venetian blind cord and was replaced by Heather Locklear Ballerina Disney 2. After Heather Locklear Ballerina Disney 2 went missing, a rule was made about selecting pet names that aren't too embarrassing to put on lost posters but it wasn't adhered to, our next cat was named Susan.

Figuring Flash might be peckish after his ordeal, I fetched a half eaten cheese sandwich from my school bag and a shallow bowl of water. He was sitting on a branch when I returned, about head height, looking decidedly better. I placed his meal at the base of the tree and stepped back. Flash stared at me for a few seconds, and then jumped down. I sat, cross-legged in the shade, watching as he took a long drink and pecked hungrily at the sandwich.

I read about another test once, an actual one, where they put a thirsty crow in a glass cage containing a pile of pebbles and a plastic tube set into the floor. The tube, half filled with water, was too narrow for the crow to get his head in to take a drink so he thought about it for a bit, then began dropping pebbles into the tube until the water level rose enough for him to get to it. This might not seem all that clever but I have coworkers that can't work out click pens.

Melissa, our secretary, once unplugged her monitor and carried it upstairs to show me an email someone had sent her, and Mike, our creative director, once kicked a hole in his office wall because he couldn't work out how to load a stapler.

Just last week, I entered the office supply room to discover Walter, our junior designer, sitting in a corner sobbing after attempting to use the spiral binder. It was upside down and hundreds of spirals were strewn all over the room so he'd obviously had a bit of a meltdown. There were a few other things going on that week that contributed to Walter's emotional state but people really need to learn to separate their personal lives from their professional lives.

"I just don't understand."
"It's really not that difficult, Walter. You punch the holes, then put the sheets into the…"
"No, I mean about my mom."
"Look, I'm sorry your mother committed suicide, Walter, but it's been two days and these reports on kitty-litter brand recognition aren't going to spiral bind themselves."

After finishing his sandwich, Flash walked a tight circle around me. I held out a hand and he retreated. I took it back and he approached, jumped onto my sneaker, and pecked at the shoelace. It was like that scene in *The Horse Whisperer* when Robert Redford, wearing a ranch jacket from his latest Sundance catalogue, whispers, "You've got this!" to a horse and they become best friends.

I haven't seen *The Horse Whisperer* but I assume that's what happens. Apparently it was a very popular movie, and I'm sure a lot of horse enthusiasts have it on Blu-ray, but the title pretty much indicates that it's not going to have robots in it. My partner Holly isn't a huge fan of movies featuring robots and movie selection is something we rarely agree on.

"Why do you always get to pick the movie we watch?"
"Because I prefer being entertained for two hours over being drawn into a pit of despair."
"What's that supposed to mean? I pick good movies."
"You pick dramas about women struggling to overcome things nobody cares about."
"Wow. That's a pretty misogynistic comment."
"No it isn't, I don't want to watch movies about men talking about their feelings either."
"I'm picking the movie. We're watching *Precious*."
"Fine. What's it about?"
"A sixteen-year-old, overweight, sexually abused black girl who lives in Harlem during the 80s. She's on welfare and has a child with Down syndrome."
"Right."
"And she catches AIDS."

Holly's pretty good at choosing Netflix series to watch though. I still complain but end up binge-watching an entire season after she falls asleep - stifling my sobs so as not to wake her as lovers run into each other's arms in airports or 1.5 lesbians dance on a stage to *Ordinary World* by Duran Duran.

I was in the kitchen making Flash another sandwich when my father pulled into the driveway. He was driving our new Ford Fairmont station wagon, brown with a lighter brown vinyl roof, purchased only four days earlier with proceeds from an insurance payout.

Our previous family car, a Leyland P76 (advertised in the mid-seventies as *The only Australian family sedan that you can fit a 44-gallon drum in the back*), had a known design flaw in which the exhaust pipe, positioned too high under the chassis, produced enough heat to set the back seat on fire. On long trips, we drove with the windows down to let out smoke and kept a gallon of water handy for when we saw flames. While stopped at traffic lights, other drivers would regularly signal for my father to wind down his window and yell that our car was on fire and he'd yell back, "Yes, I'm fully aware of that. Why don't you mind your own fucking business?"

My father hated the P76 but refused to say so; conceding that he had bought a lemon would be admitting to a mistake and my father never made mistakes. Once, during a family road trip across Australia, he drove six hundred miles in the wrong direction and blamed my mother for folding the roadmap wrong.

"You have to fold it in the middle, then over, then across twice... no wait... over, then over again, then across twice, then over again."
"What does it matter?"
"The creases go the wrong way if you don't fold it properly."
"Why don't you just admit you missed the turnoff?"
"It was in a crease. Facing the wrong way."

I didn't know at the time that my father hated the P76, his immutable over-compensating praise for the deathtrap led me to believe that the vehicle's tendency to catch fire was simply a feature that worked too well. It did keep the vehicle warm in winter. Then, one particularly warm summer afternoon, my father left the car running with the AC on while we shopped in Target. He said it was so the car would be cool when we got back, but he'd never done it before. As we left the store and made our way towards the parking lot, we saw smoke and heard distant sirens. My father did a little fist punch at his side before quickly containing his elation.

"Oh no. Our car is on fire. It's a terrible thing! It's unsafe to approach so there's nothing we can do but stand well back and let the fire take its course."

I'm paraphrasing but the presentation was actually far more melodramatic and included a whole speech about his family's safety being more important than a car and, after a crowd had gathered, shaking his fist at the sky and asking Jesus how this could have happened.

I'd wondered on the drive to Target why there was a stack of odd-smelling newspapers on the back seat - and why my father ejected his Bee Gee's *Stayin' Alive* cassingle and took it into the store with him - but I guess I was too excited about the impromptu trip to buy beanbags to query.

I'm not accusing my father of insurance fraud but a claim investigator did. The company only agreed to compensation after my father threatened to call *60 Minutes* about their refusal to pay an honest, hard-working, family man and used the term 'habeas corpus' incorrectly a dozen times.

"I mean, why would I buy four beanbags* if I knew the car was going to catch fire? We had to carry them home on the bus. Habeas corpus!"

It was a valid argument. Boarding the bus with my family, each of us carrying a beanbag, was honestly mortifying. People pointed, a few chuckled. My father loudly instructed us several times not to let our beanbags touch anything because we might get a rip. A kid from my school was on the bus so everyone in my class knew about it the next day.

My father refused to admit that he hated the P76 even after it was replaced. He loved the new station wagon with

---

* *Our sofa broke and rather than replace it, my father decided to buy four beanbags. Later, we bought another two for guests. The original four were green vinyl but Target had run out of that color when we went back to get more so the guest beanbags were orange. It made them easy to tell apart and when my sister or I sat on them, my father would yell, "Get off the good beanbags, they're only for guests."*

a passion - he'd washed and polished 'Brown Beauty' twice in as many days - but he was careful to end any sentence praising Brown Beauty's features with a balanced 'tip of the hat' to the P76.

"Listen to this... four speakers instead of just one in the dash. You can actually hear Barry Gibb taking a quick breath between lyrics. It's like he's in the car with you. Of course the P76 had its advantages as well, did you know it's the only Australian sedan that can fit a 44-gallon drum in the back?"
"Why would anyone want to?"
"That's not the point. The point is, if someone wanted to, they could."
"It just seems like an odd selling point."
"Not at all, 44-gallon drums are very handy. If you drill a dozen or so holes in the side, they make a terrific backyard incinerator."
"Still, a niché market. Besides, you could probably fit two of them in the new station wagon."
"Why would anyone need *two* 44-gallon drums?"

My offspring Seb and I actually purchased a 44-gallon drum from a guy on Craigslist last autumn. It was fifteen dollars and fit easily in the back of our Jeep. We drilled a dozen or so holes in the side, packed it with dead leaves, and, after instructing Seb to add a splash of fuel from a jerry can, I went inside to get a lighter.

"How much fuel did you put in?"
"A splash."
"The jerry-can is empty."
"A decent splash."

I expected a 'whoompf' but I didn't expect the volume, or for the drum to act like a cannon. Burning leaves shot high into the air and rained down over a four hundred foot radius. There was a fair amount of screaming and running. Seb lost a new t-shirt to a burn hole, which he was rather upset about, but I refused to drive him to the mall to replace it.

"We have to go, Pacsun will sell out of these shirts and I'll never find another one with pineapples on the pocket."
"You should have thought about that before dumping several gallons of fuel into the 44-gallon drum. I'm not leaving the house for four or five weeks."
"Oh my god, Dad, it's not even that noticeable. Just draw on eyebrows with a marker and wear a hat."
"Yes, that's an excellent suggestion, Seb. Perhaps a snappy vest and a cane to complete the ensemble."
"Your hair's not even that bad. Just short at the front."
"I have *no* hair at the front. It's just little frizzle-balls. I look like an old Chinese man that works on a wharf. All I need is a couple of big sacks on my back."
"Shave it all off then. You'll look like Jason Statham."
"You really think so?"
"...Sure."

The problem is that some people's heads are Jason Statham shaped and others are concentration camp prisoner shaped. You never really know what shape your head is, or how white, until you go #0 with a set of Wahl dog grooming clippers. I'd watched a movie a few nights before, called *The Descent*, about a group of women who go spelunking without spare flashlight batteries and get chased by pale, bald humanoid creatures that live in the dark. I watched it by myself and there were a lot of jump scares, which explains why, for two or three days after shaving my head, I'd yell and go all wobbly whenever I passed a mirror.

"I don't look anything like Jason Statham."
"Yes, you do. If he had no muscles and was maybe sick."
"If he was sick?"
"Cancer or something. Can we go to Pacsun now?"

Later, we learned our neighbor Carl had recorded the entire 'rain of fire' incident on his phone and presented the video during that week's sub-division HOA meeting. Apparently it's against the rules to burn rubbish in your backyard because a horse burnt to death in 1876. The fine is a shiny shilling or forfeiture of your least-unattractive daughter to the town's elders. There are also ordinances covering pitching your neighbor's well, rolling your sleeves above the elbow while churning butter, and, for the record, mowing your lawn after 7pm and before 9am. Also, nobody is allowed to own chickens.

Conveniently, Carl 'my mower has headlights' Mishler is the president of our sub-division HOA and there are only two other members: Carl's short, round, curly-haired wife Toni, who seconds every motion, and Janice Roberts, a 93 year-old semi-mobile corpse from across the street who owns chickens and has a large sign in her front yard that states, *Though I may stumble, I will not fall, for the Lord upholds me with his hand. Psalms 37:23.* Which is false, as I've seen Janice fall at least three times. Despite a decade or two of using a walker, it's as though each outing is the first time she's ever seen one; there's no 'lift, place, step, repeat' rhythm, its just random flailing and clanking. I saw her using it upside down once, she was holding onto the tennis balls. On one occasion, she somehow managed to throw the walker twenty feet ahead, fell, and couldn't get up for several minutes. I would have eventually helped but a UPS driver stopped and lifted her off the road before I finished my coffee.

According to the written warning I received (signed, countersigned and witnessed by Carl, Toni and Janice), it was the sixth recorded instance of Seb and I breaking HOA ordinances. Some of Carl's earlier work included, *Thorne's riding ATVs on the road*, *Thorne's feeding raccoons*, and, my personal favourite, *Thorne's rolling a log down a hill into a creek*.

I emailed the HOA my own video footage (an animated gif titled *Carl_sucking_horse_cock*) but they didn't respond.

The morning my father bought Brown Beauty home, my sister and I were given a lengthy list of instructions. These included the standard 'no food or drinks' and 'no muddy shoes' rules, but also several that pushed the point a little far such as 'hair must be washed before using the headrests' and 'occupants must wear a plastic trash bag with a head hole cut out of it if they have played with the dog.' 'Hands must be clasped in your lap at all times' was included to stop anyone picking at or removing the factory plastic protecting the vinyl seats, but remained in effect even after my father purchased plastic protective seat covers to protect the factory protective plastic.

Once, my father drove to collect me from basketball practice but because I was a bit sweaty, gave me bus fare instead and drove off. I was eight and had never ridden public transport by myself. An old guy sat next to me on the bus and suggested I get off at his stop to see his Apple II computer so I could easily have been molested. I wasn't though, we just played *Lode Runner* and ate chips for a few hours. I actually visited his house several times after that before I was molested.*

---

* *Molested is probably too strong a term – there was no penetration or sucking, he simply wanted us to take turns placing our penises onto a piece of paper and tracing around them with a pen. Apparently I did it wrong so he had to trace mine for me a couple of times. The trick is to pull the foreskin back so you have a more defined edge to trace; otherwise it just looks like a mushroom with a bump.*

Pride of ownership isn't a negative trait of course, the extreme opposite is worse. We moved recently - to get the fuck away from Carl - and our new neighbours, a dwarf and his blurry wife, have embraced 'extreme opposite' to the point where their house should probably just be bulldozed. He might not actually be a dwarf, it's possible he's just really short with weird chubby arms and legs. And his wife isn't actually blurry, just so nondescript that ten seconds after seeing her, I forget what she looks like. I think she has straight brown hair. Also, her name might be Karen. Or Jill. I don't care. Apparently they're artists but I've known artists who were capable of using a weed whacker. It's not all just about wearing black and bringing rusty benches home from the dump to put on your front lawn. A rusty dump-bench doesn't say, "Look at how bohemian we are", it says, "Fuck you, we're taking everyone's property value down with us."

The crackhouse-chique theme isn't restrained to the exterior either; Dwarf and Blurry don't own blinds so at night, we get the full experience of what it would be like to live in a third-world country. At some point, one of them must have declared, "You know what would make great living room furniture? A beige plastic outdoor setting from Wal-Mart. And I'll paint it without primer." To which the other no doubt answered, "Great idea, it will go perfectly with our cinder-block bookcase and the six-foot papier-mâché giraffe we found in a dumpster behind Pier-1."

Also, I once saw the blurry wife dancing in a poncho while the dwarf played bongos. It must have been a bongo song about birds because she was flapping her poncho like wings.

It's easy to be judgmental. Really easy. I'd probably still bother if it took effort though. I'd have nothing to talk about otherwise.

"I see your neighbors have put a bench on their front lawn."
"Yes, a metal one. Looks great."
"Really, David?"
"Yes, it's very bohemian. They're artists, did you know?"
"It's covered in rust."
"Ah, yes, the patina. So much character. You won't find that on West Elm patio furniture."
"It's an eyesore. And weird. Who puts an old rusty bench in the middle of their front lawn facing the street? Are they planning to sit on it and wave to people passing by?"
"I do hope so. The neighborly wave is sadly uncommon nowadays."
"You're behaving oddly and there's a large vein on your forehead that looks like it's about to burst."
"Yes, I'm having a stroke."

Holly and I actually play a game called 'The Judgmental Game' which we made up and somehow don't feel bad about. Basically, if you're driving along and you see someone wearing, for example, terry toweling, you declare, "Hey, there's Terry!" and the other person has to guess Terry's last name - which in this instance is obviously Toweling. Just this afternoon, on the way to the supermarket, we passed Roger Redpants and argued whether Erin Electric Scooter counts because it was a bit of a stretch. Holly's not very good at the game.

"Hey, there's Sally!"
"Hmm... Sally who?"
"Sally Shopping Cart."
"We all have shopping carts, Holly. We're shopping in a supermarket."
"And? Hey, there's Sue!"
"Sue Shopping Cart?"
"No, Sue Williams. I went to school with her sister."

Ideally, a middle ground between obsessive pride and the extreme opposite needs to be found. Somewhere 'normal' between rusty dump-benches and declaring war on birds...

On the third morning of ownership, my father discovered a bird dropping splatter on Brown Beauty. It was just one, and not very large, but as far as my father was concerned, it was deliberate and malicious vandalism - like kicking a hole in the *Mona Lisa* or putting a piece of sticky-tape over the tab on a certain cassingle and recording yourself singing the theme to *The Greatest American Hero*.

My punishment for recording over *Stayin' Alive* was to stand at the entrance of our driveway holding a sign that read, "I have no respect for other people's property." I also wasn't allowed to watch *The Greatest American Hero* again so I have no idea if the curly blonde guy eventually worked out how to land without hitting billboards. Holding a sign was a common punishment in our household and I'd informed the neighborhood of several offences over the years, including: "I stole $10 from my mother's purse to buy a plastic sword", "I swapped my sister's bike for 3 Penthouse magazines", and, "Honk if you dislike liars; I told my teacher my parents died."

Our house had an attached garage but, a few years earlier, it had been converted into a 'granny-flat' for my mother's sister, Auntie Brenda, to stay in after she became terminally ill. It wasn't much of a conversion, my father did the work himself, but it had a bed and basic amenities.

My father was originally against the conversion. He and Auntie Brenda had physically scuffled once during a family Christmas dinner after he called her a "disgusting bushpig" for chewing with her mouth open, and she spat a mouthful of stuffing and cranberry sauce at his face in response. His favorite white Lacoste polo shirt was ruined. He sent Auntie Brenda an invoice for replacement, with follow-up reminders and a final notice, but she never paid it.

The conversion only went ahead after my mother agreed it could become a man-cave when Auntie Brenda died. My father bought a framed print of dogs playing poker and a neon beer clock in anticipation.

Auntie Brenda was originally given six months to live but lasted three years. I'm not sure what her illness was but she lost her hair and coughed a lot. Often she'd cough until she soiled herself and there was a special basket in our laundry for her bedding with an airtight lid. Sometimes my sister would remove the basket lid and lock me in the laundry. Once, she threw a used adult diaper at me and urine went in my mouth. Which isn't relative to the story in any way, I just want it on record. I've not mentioned the incident since as I'm waiting for the right moment.

"David, the doctors have given me less than two weeks to live if I don't find a donor kidney match. I know it's a big ask but, as my brother, I was wondering..."
"Remember when you threw a used adult diaper at me?"
"What?"
"Urine went in my mouth. Auntie Brenda's urine."
"Okay..."
"It was quite upsetting at the time. I thought it meant I had whatever she had. I wrote a will."
"I don't..."
"Something to think about as your dialysis machine fails and you convulse to death."

As she was bedridden, we didn't see much of Auntie Brenda but we heard her often. During particularly bad coughing fits, my father would pound on the adjoining wall and yell, "I'm trying to watch TV in here, just fucking die already!" and she'd yell back, "Fuck you, monkey!" - a reference to my father's long sideburns. He shaved the sideburns off the day after she died so I suspect the name bothered him only slightly less than having Auntie Brenda know it bothered him at all.

I remember the evening Auntie Brenda died, we were watching *Magnum PI* and my father said, "Haven't heard Golum hacking up a lung in a while, better go and check on her, David."

She was naked, hanging half off the bed, a large, wet fecal stain beneath her hips. I'd never seen naked breasts before so I gave one a squeeze.

I'm joking about squeezing Auntie Brenda's breast. I wasn't even the one who discovered her. I only added the above paragraph because I imagined the look on Holly's face as she proofreads it. I'll delete it before this book goes to print (unless I forget or it messes up my formatting), otherwise I'll receive dozens of annoying emails from the elderly, angry at the world about their shingles and the price of irritable bowel medicine, asking what, exactly, is amusing about molesting a dead relative.

It was my sister who checked on Auntie Brenda. She had nightmares for years afterwards and refused to go into the converted garage even after my father took the bed to the dump and put a bar, television, dart board, and two beanbags in there. For a while, he had a poster behind the bar of Kelly LeBrock sitting on a moped in a bikini but my mother ripped it down during an argument about having her sewing table and chair in the man cave.

"Why can't it be the 'family cave'?"
"We already have a family cave, it's called the living room. This is my area to get away from everyone."
"Well perhaps I'd like my own area to get away from everyone as well."
"You already have one."
"Where?"
"The kitchen."
"..."
"You're welcome to visit though."

A few days after the argument, while my mother was at the supermarket, my father cleaned out the tool shed, ran an extension cord from the house, and put her sewing table and chair in there. He also put a piece of green carpet on the concrete floor and hung a painting of two kittens playing with yarn on a wall. I'm sure he expected my mother to be delighted but, after being led outside in a blindfold for the reveal, she locked herself in the bathroom and cried.

My father hung his neon clock where the Kelly LeBrock poster had been. It said 'Beer o'clock' on it and had glasses of beer instead of numbers. He also put an old fridge (rescued from the dump along with two golf cart wheels and a painting of two kittens playing with yarn) in the man cave. It rattled and hummed loudly but kept beer cold until a collection of magazines he'd hidden behind it caught fire. There wasn't an extensive amount of damage* but a section of linoleum, the framed print of dogs playing poker, a cricket bat signed by Merv Hughes, and a beanbag was lost. I was quietly sad about the magazines as I'd known about them for months and was smitten with March 1982's playmate of the month, Karen Witter. Really we had Karen to thank for the fire being discovered before it did more damage.

Mumbling the whole time about uric acid damage, my father washed and polished Brown Beauty again, then carried a beanbag out to the driveway and sat guard. Whenever a bird approached, he'd leap up and wave his arms about while yelling obscenities. It was a hot day and the cricket was on television so he only kept it up for about twenty minutes before it was my turn.

---

* *Two lengths of water pipe, which my father installed during the garage conversion, were joined with a piece of vacuum cleaner hose and duct tape. The join, inside the wall that the refrigerator was against, had leaked steadily over three years and the inch-thick sheet of black mold behind the drywall was far too wet to burn.*

"You're not waving your arms fast enough."
"Yes I am."
"I was watching through the window. A bird landed on the fence and it didn't give a fuck about your slow-motion arm waving. You didn't even get out of the beanbag."
"How long do I have to do this for?"
"Why, do you have a meeting to go to?"
"No."
"Well, there you go. Bird!"
"Where?"
"It flew over."
"I can't stop birds from flying over the house."
"No, not with that attitude. I'm taking the beanbag back inside."

"Do you have a meeting to go to?" was one of my father's favorite things to say whenever I questioned doing something or going somewhere. Equally annoying variations included, "Are you wanted in surgery? I didn't hear your beeper go off." and, "Do you have a plane to catch, Mr Allen? Are you going to Rio?"

Crows are not only highly intelligent, they are also highly social. If a crow is out and about and comes across a decent meal - a dead cat or something - it heads back to wherever crows hang out, tells a group of friends, and they all head to the dead cat together - where they take turns to peck. If one of them gets a bit greedy and pushes in, that crow will be admonished by the group, made to stand several steps back, and miss a turn. It's a decidedly ordered social practice that should be adopted in workplaces whenever anyone brings in cake.

"Back off Jodie,* you can't have a second piece before everyone has received their first. There are societal rules and you have broken them."
"I understand and apologize. I will now take several steps back and miss a turn."

Crows will also invite their friends to a fight. It's like throwing a motorcycle club member out of a bar and having his entire gang turn up thirty minutes later.

I was in a biker-brawl once. Not as one of the motorcycle club members, just as a participant, there's no way I'd ever be seen in public wearing a denim jacket with the sleeves cut off. I had a stonewash denim jacket in the eighties but it had sleeves.

---

* *Unlike a crow, there's no way that my coworker Jodie, happening upon cake in the kitchen area, would alert others to the fact. She'd quietly lock the door and shovel cake into her gob with both hands. Afterwards, she'd send an email to all staff stating, "Not sure who bought cake in today but unfortunately it fell on the ground and had to be thrown it in the trash. Can people please not leave their coffee mugs on the kitchen bench as it doesn't leave much room for food. Thanks, Jodie."***

** *That's right, Jodie, nobody fell for that bullshit.*

I was working at de Masi jones at the time*, a small branding agency in Adelaide, Australia. It was the creative director's birthday and we'd knocked off early to have drinks at a new bar called The Garage. It was a 'hole in the wall' bar but the proprietor had installed wall-to-wall mirrors to make it feel four times as roomy. A fair amount of money had also been spent on theming it with a 1950's fuel pump and service-station related signage but, because of the mirrors, it kind of felt like it had all been plonked down in the middle of a tiny dance studio.

Being around four in the afternoon, there were only a handful of patrons: our group of five, a young couple, two or three hat-wearing hipsters, and an old guy wearing a denim jacket with the sleeves cut off. The old guy, crouched over the bar cradling a pint of Cooper's Sparkling Ale, had a long grey beard and was mostly bald apart from a little braided plait at the back like Anakin Skywalker's. A poorly drawn skull and wiggly typeface on the back of his sleeveless jacket declared him to be a member of the Gypsy Jokers.

My only previous experience with a biker gang was when God's Squad, an Australian Christian motorcycle club, came to my school in fifth grade to tell us how cool it is to love Jesus.

---

* *At the time of the brawl, not during my stonewash denim phase.*

One of the God's Squad members told a story about how he used to steal copper wiring from construction sites until he had a dream about holding hands with Jesus, and a couple of biker-chicks danced to an Amy Grant song. It pretty much established for me the fact that loving Jesus isn't cool.

I approached the bar, a few stools down from the old guy, and ordered the same beer as he was drinking.
"Good choice," he slurred, raising his beer in salute. I smiled and gave an agreeing nod. There was an awkward wait as the bartender, a petite girl with pink hair, poured my beer.
"What type of bike do you ride?" I asked. It was the motorcycle-related equivalent of 'The elevator's certainly taking its time' or 'Still raining? Can't trust anything the weatherman says'.
"An 02 Triumph Bonneville," he answered.
"Nice. I've got a Honda at home." I didn't, but I'd owned one years before. It was a 75cc postman's scooter.
"The Gold Wing?"
"No, just the normal wing, I'm not a huge fan of bling."
"..."
"Yes, there's nothing like being out on the wide open road on a hog. Love to ride, ride to survive as they say."
"It's 'live to ride, ride to live'."
"Is it? Still, it's the same message - enjoy the trip but stay safe. Especially if it's wet out."

The birthday boy, Thomas de Masi, was in the process of opening his brightly wrapped present when I sat at our group's table. We'd all chipped in ten dollars but I'd picked it out. It was quite a thoughtful gift so everybody's reaction to the coffee mug with *World's Greatest Boss* written on it was a bit disappointing. It's the thought that counts and I don't recall anyone mentioning an electric beard-grooming kit. They demanded their money back but I'd already spent it on bed sheets.

We were on our third drink when the commotion started. The old guy ordered another beer and the girl with the pink hair suggested he'd had enough. There was a heated exchange, during which the term 'cunt faced dyke' was used, and the bouncer, a large black guy wearing a shirt two sizes too small, asked the old guy to leave. The scuffle was brief - the old guy swung and missed, found himself in a headlock, and was dragged out the door.

I'd estimate it was slightly less than thirty minutes before the old guy returned with his friends as it takes Thomas thirty minutes to tell his five-minute shemale story and he was only up to the part about rubbing what he thought was large labia through panties when the front window shattered inwards. The bikers, at least a dozen of them, swarmed in like cockroaches. Later, it was difficult to give the police an accurate account of the next few minutes as everything happened at once in one terrifying barrage of noise and violence.

The bouncer managed to get in a few good punches before he went down. The 1950's fuel pump was thrown over the bar, taking out three shelves of bottles and the mirror behind them. The pink haired bartender took a stool to the face and went backwards in a spray of blood. The hipsters locked themselves in a bathroom and the young couple hid under their table. Thomas ducked to join them as one of the bikers, wielding a huge spanner, headed menacingly towards our group. He half raised his weapon and stopped, nodded. I nodded back at the old guy in the sleeveless denim jacket, picked up the *World's Greatest Boss* mug, and threw it at a wall-mirror.

It wasn't my proudest moment and I left that bit out in the police report, but, just for an instant, it felt kind of nice to be part of a club. There was a camaraderie, an understanding, a shared love of being out on the wide open road on a hog. It's probably the same way knitting club members feel about yarn or Rotary Club members feel about manicured barbecue areas.

I've only ever been a member of two clubs, the Kiss Army, which had no club meetings, just stickers, and the Tea Tree Gully Tennis Club which I stopped attending after the head coach, Mister Jobs, hit a tennis ball really hard at me for jokingly calling him 'Head Jobs'. It hurt a lot and I was embarrassed in front of several kids so I walked off the court, knocked the driver's side mirror off his Toyota Corolla with three or four swings of my tennis racquet, and ran. My father had to pay for the damage and I had to change Auntie Brenda's sheets for a week as punishment.

My friend JM is in a club called the Elk's Lodge and he invited me to a meeting once. I'd assumed it was some kind of vacation timeshare in the mountains and that I was going to be offered a few nights free stay in exchange for listening to a short presentation but it turned out to be a bunch of elderly men in ill-fitting suits standing in a room eating luncheon meats and sharing hip-surgery updates. One of the elderly men gave me a twenty-minute detailed account of his trip to Target to buy a toaster earlier that day and another scolded me for being Australian. Apparently he knew an Australian named Bill during the war, possibly the Civil War, who stole his watch while he was sleeping. It was a watch that his father had given him that his father's father had given his father... I phased out after five minutes but from what I could tell, the watch had been handed down since sometime during the Mesozoic period. Not having Bill's side of the story, I suggested that the watch may have been lost and was met with a slammed down plate of luncheon meats and the yelled rebuttal, "It was on a chain!"

After everyone had finished their luncheon meats, they led a naked young man wearing an elk mask into the middle of the room, formed a circle around him while removing their pants, and took turns giving him their seed as the group made grunting noises and chanted, "We are bigger elks!"

I left before the ritual but I'm pretty sure that's what happens. I didn't go to any more meetings because JM told me that once a year, members have to go door-to-door selling brooms for deaf kids or something.

Unfortunately, the incident at The Garage was captured on surveillance video and shown on the local news the next night. The footage was grainy but they zoomed in for the mug bit.

From: Geoffrey Peters
Date: Thursday 17 August 2006 8.02pm
To: David Thorne
Subject: Channel 7 news

Tell me that wasn't you throwing a coffee mug at a mirror on the news tonight.

From: David Thorne
Date: Thursday 17 August 2006 8.46pm
To: Geoffrey Peters
Subject: Re. Channel 7 news

It was a survival situation and spur of the moment decision.

From: Geoffrey Peters
Date: Thursday 17 August 2006 9.17pm
To: David Thorne
Subject: Re. Re. Channel 7 news

You hugged one of the bikers afterwards. Hey, can you give me a lift to my Medieval Society meetup tomorrow? I can't catch the bus in chainmail because I can't use the step.

....

I received several similar emails the next morning. One was from a guy I bought a laptop from three years prior and had met for ten-minutes, four were from clients. I told the marketing manager of McDonald's Australia that I had an identical twin named Douglas.

Thinking I might be arrested, I turned myself in at the local police station that afternoon. I was interviewed in a room by two officers but, after viewing the footage together, I was told there wouldn't be any charges and I could leave. On my way out, I heard one the officers yell, "Mike, get in here and watch this, it's fucking hilarious," and someone, I assume Mike, yell back, "Is it the video where the guy throws a mug? I've seen it."

I saw the girl with pink hair a few weeks later; she was working at another bar and had a large bandage across her nose. I asked her out but she said no.

I heard my father yelling. He yelled a lot so I didn't pay it much attention; he yelled at people on television, at ants, at dry patches of lawn. He once yelled at the ocean after being knocked over by wave. I took my time finishing Flash's sandwich, cutting it into four small triangles with the crusts removed, before heading outside.

There were five crows sitting in the branches of the single large maple that shaded the driveway. I'm not sure which one was Flash. They stared down at my father, unperturbed by his yelling and arm waving, until he picked up a rock and threw it.

It was a fairly hefty rock, large enough to hide a spare front door key under. It had, in fact, once been the designated 'spare key rock' but my mother lifted it one day after locking herself out of the house and a spider ran up her arm. After that, the key was kept in a jar behind the shed until it was required again and my mother was bitten by a snake. It was non-venomous but nobody knew that at the time. My mother must have once seen an episode of *The Lone Ranger* or something because she asked my father to suck out the poison and he replied, "No point in both of us being poisoned." After that, the key was kept under the front door mat until it went missing one day and my father had the locks changed because he was adamant someone had stolen it and we were all going to be murdered in our sleep. When we moved, years later, we found it under the washing machine.

My father later claimed he hadn't aimed at the crows, that it was intended as a warning shot, but my yell for him to stop had distracted him mid-throw, causing the direct hit. With a flurry of feathers and alarmed caws, four of the crows hit the air and one hit the ground.

When I was in fifth grade, George Papadopoulos threw a rock at me while I was riding my bike home from school. I'm not sure what his issue with me was but he was Greek and most Greek people I've met have been the type to throw rocks at kids for no reason. That's not being racist, Greek people aren't black, it's just that the whole "We invented philosophy!" attitude while they're painting your house or wrapping rice in soggy grape leaves gets a bit old. Yemen invented coffee but I can get a decent coffee anywhere without contracting cholera.*

Also, concreting your front lawn and adding columns doesn't make your suburban three bedroom brick house the Parthenon. I get that concrete is a symbol of status to Greek people - the more columns, ponds and statues in their yard, the higher their social ranking - but for everyone else living on the street, it's an eyesore that should be bulldozed. We had a lot of Greeks in our neighborhood. Our next-door neighbor, Mr Kostas, was

---

Yemen's currency is bottled water and its tourism slogan is "Visit Yemen. We wear suit jackets in rubble."

Greek and his perpetual concrete-based landscaping infuriated my father.

"Give it a fucking rest, Dennis! You can't run a cement mixer after 7pm. It's a city ordinance."
"Fuck you, Philip!"
"No, fuck you, Dennis. I'll call the cops."
"If you call the cops on me, you call the cops on my whole family."
"You're not the fucking Godfather, Dennis."
The Kostas are well respected in the community."
"Not around here, dickhead. We all think your front yard looks like shit."
"My front yard is beautiful. Your front yard looks like shit."
"At least I've got lawn, Dennis. Lawn!"

The rock struck my head with some force, just above my ear, and I fell off my bike. Granted it was a good shot - it's not easy to hit a moving target from across the street - but the way George cheered and carried on, you'd think he'd just won a lifetime supply of tzatziki in a contest.

Lifting myself to my feet, I touched the side of my head and felt wet hair. There was blood on my fingertips and I held the hand up to show George.
"You're in big trouble," I shouted, "I'm bleeding!"
"Good!" George shouted back, bending down to pick up another rock.

I was in disbelief. The interaction had resulted in blood which is when both parties go their separate ways with shouted, sometimes tearful, 'over the shoulder' reiteration of how much trouble the other person is in. It's the rules. Instead, George threw another rock. I ducked and it whistled past my ear and struck a fence.

As I was only three or four houses down from where I lived, I had the option - the sensible option - to grab my bike and run with it to the safety of my driveway, but outrage won over self preservation. It was like that scene in every action movie ever made where the underdog, bloody and beaten, stands in slow-motion to face his opponent, usually with a close-up of a fist being clenched and narrowing eyes. Except in this instance, crying and searching desperately for a rock.

George's side of the road had better ammunition than my side, the yard he was in front of had an entire rock garden to select from. A fence blocked the yard on my side but there was a rusty circular metal plate set into the sidewalk. It was approximately six inches in radius, about the size of a discus, with the words *South Australian Water Corporation* stamped around the edge. It was raised on one side, with a gap large enough to get my fingers under, and I pried it up easily. Having taken part in the discus throw during 'sports days' at school a few times, I knew the basic technique; holding the metal plate at arms length, I spun around and released with all my strength.

In the heat of battle, I hadn't checked if any vehicles were coming. The driver of the white van lost control when the metal plate crashed through his passenger side window. He careened left and right for almost a hundred feet before mounting the sidewalk and crashing into Mr Kostas front yard, taking out a statue of Aphrodite.

It was pretty much the most trouble I had ever been in up to that point. The police were involved and there was an ambulance at Mr Kostas' house for a time. The driver of the van didn't require hospitalization but when Aphrodite's head went through the windshield, pieces of glass cut his arm badly enough to need a bandage. Mr Kostas was pretty upset but I don't know what he called me as it was in Greek.

George had bolted seconds after the crash. It wasn't him who had thrown the metal plate so his part in the event wasn't of any interest to the police, but when he approached me at school the next day to inquire what happened after he left, I told him the police knew it was all his fault, had an APB out for his arrest, and he was looking at ten years because the driver died. He said he didn't believe me but when a police car drove past the school with its siren on during recess, he hid in the bathroom. I asked an older kid to pound on the door and yell, "Police! Come out with your hands up!" but George had already climbed out a window and gone home.

I wasn't charged but I had to meet a social worker at the local library who asked me about the incident and made me watch a short video called *Our Community* about a kid who vandalizes a phone booth but then needs to call his mother to pick him up but can't so he sleeps in a hedge in someone's front yard. I was also grounded and had television privileges revoked for six months. It was a difficult six months because *Knight Rider* first aired during that time. It was all anyone at school talked about and George wore a KITT t-shirt to school one day, which rubbed it in a bit. While the rest of my family was enjoying the adventures of an advanced artificially intelligent, self-aware car, I was mixing concrete in Mr Kostas' front yard to pay for damages.

I learned a lot about traditional Greek concrete mixing formulas during that time - the secret is to add two glasses of full-cream milk to each batch so the concrete doesn't crack as it sets. By the end of the six months, we'd completed a 10'x8' raised pond with steps leading up to it and a triple-tiered water feature. During summer evenings, Mr Kostas and I would often sit by it eating cheese and grapes from a wooden platter.

George was eventually expelled from school, for selling bags of dried basil under the guise of marijuana from his locker, but I saw him several years later at University. He still had his hair styled like Michael Knight's and was on a ladder with a paint roller.

I buried the dead crow in the backyard next to Heather Locklear Ballerina Disney, Heather Locklear Ballerina Disney 2, Henry, and Susan. Susan had died when a sheet of metal roofing my father was replacing fell and cut her in half.* Henry was a tortoise my father backed over with the car. I wrote *Flash!* on a piece of wood and used it as a tombstone. I wasn't positive it was him but Flash had been friendly and the fifty or so crows now stationed in the front yard were really mean.

Our front yard looked like a scene from that Hitchcock movie about angry birds. Except in colour and without women with beehives screaming while doing jazz fingers. There were crows in the maple, crows on the fence, and crows on overhead wires. My father tried using the garden hose to scare them off but we hadn't had decent water pressure since the garage conversion and the light spray just seemed to invigorate them.

Several swooped, or one swooped several times, it's hard to tell with crows. My father ducked and wove like he was plugged into the Matrix but an especially close attack clipped his ear.

---

* *It didn't cut her completely in half. There was still about an inch of flesh holding Susan's two halves together and she didn't die instantly. She managed to drag herself several feet in the time it took my father to climb down from the roof and finish her off with a shovel.*

Retreating momentarily, he ditched the hose and grabbed a rake, running back into battle with it held high like a sword. The crows took to the highest branches and overhead wires to regroup.

For several minutes, they watched silently as my father circled Brown Beauty below, waving his rake back and forth like a flag bearer in a parade... Watched as he stopped to wipe a bird dropping off the windshield with a handkerchief and shake a fist up at them.

Something clicked.

A single crow cawed, another answered. Several joined in the discussion as if in agreement. They understood what my father was waging this war over, what he was trying to protect, what would exact the most vengeance.

Within the hour, Brown Beauty looked like it had been shot up with white paintballs. A wiper blade had been ripped off, both side mirrors were cracked, and the second F from the Ford Fairmont lettering was missing. My father watched from the living room window, nursing both his ear and a new wound on the top of his head where a crow had pecked out a small chunk of flesh. It must have hurt a lot because it was the first time I'd ever heard my father scream. The chunk was still attached but he had to push it back into the hole and hold a towel to his head to stem the bleeding.

Later, the chunk actually rotted and he had to have surgery to remove a two-inch section of his scalp due to gangrene setting in. My father wasn't a fan of going to the doctor* but after my mother complained about the smell for two weeks, he finally relented to getting it looked at. If he'd left it much longer, he probably would have lost his whole head. Also, a couple of nights after the surgery, the dressing fell off while my father was sleeping and when he awoke the next morning, my mother had to drive him back to the hospital with a pillow stuck to his head.

The crows called a ceasefire at dusk and their numbers dwindled as they headed off to roost for the night. By that time, Brown Beauty's Ford Fairmont lettering just said *ont*, a hubcap was gone, and the antenna had been pulled out of its mounting hole. Stripped wires dangled from the hole and the antenna dangled from a tree branch. Their claws had also made short work of the paintwork; it looked like a thousand tiny Canadians had practiced curling with dinner forks.

---

* *He once shot a hole through his hand with an industrial nail-gun and fixed it with wood-putty. Another time, during a camping trip, he ripped a gash in his leg while collecting firewood and fixed it with duct tape. He complained that the gash itched but, as the tape was stuck firmly to his hairy legs, he left it on for a week until he saw a termite crawl out from under it. Ignoring suggestions to seek medical advice, he sprayed insect-spray into the wound and put another piece of duct tape over it.*

They returned in force the next morning but Brown Beauty wasn't in the driveway. Anticipating their return, my father drove, under cover of darkness, several hundred feet down the street and parked the vehicle in front of an empty lot. Someone broke in and stole the stereo that night but if he hadn't moved it, the crows would have probably taken the stereo anyway. With nothing to focus their retribution on, the crows eventually got bored and left.

Mr Kostas found the hubcap in his pond but the rest of the repairs came to well over three thousand dollars. Despite my father declaring habeas corpus several times and stating that he was best friends with the guys on *60 Minutes*, the insurance company denied coverage as their policy listed bird damage as a natural event. He asked if turning up at their office with an axe and killing everyone would be considered a natural extension of a natural event and a couple of police officers spoke to him about it later that evening.

The repair shop did a good job and Brown Beauty looked like it had when my father first brought it home. He purchased a car cover and, for several months, was anal about putting it on whenever the car wasn't being used. Even if we were just shopping at a supermarket, we'd all have to wait while he positioned it perfectly and secured it with Velcro straps. Leaving wasn't any quicker as the cover had to be folded correctly and stored in its bag.

Eventually, as the new-car-smell faded and the protective plastic seat covers that protected the factory protective plastic seat covers tore, my father didn't put the car cover on quite as often and he stopped using the velcro straps altogether.

When a gust of wind caught the cover, during a blustery shopping trip to buy my sister and I sneakers, he didn't bother asking for a ladder to retrieve it from the top of a Kmart sign and he didn't replace it. It flapped there for two months before someone removed it. Sometimes the breeze would catch it at just the right angle and it looked like the big red letter K was wearing a beret. You'd think the manager might have cared enough to have it removed but I know a guy named Gavin who is the manager of a Kmart and he's far too busy with in-store operations to be concerned with the exterior. Those iPads, wide-screen televisions and kitchen appliances aren't going to hop into the back of his car by themselves. I bought a microwave oven from him for $25 last week and the recommended retail price is $79.90 plus tax.

And yes, my sister and I had to wear sneakers from Kmart when we were young. While the other kids at school were sporting black Adidas Koln II's and Reebok Pumps, I was rocking Dunlop Volley knockoffs that said Doing Laps on the heel.

My father picked me up after basketball practice one day and I pointed out a bird dropping splatter on the roof. He took Brown Beauty through a carwash on the way home, which is something he never did because they do a half-arsed job and scratch the clear-coat. Yes, even the brushless ones. I know someone who drove their Daihatsu through a brushless car wash and the water pressure dented two door panels and took the paint off the bumpers. Granted Daihatsu make their cars out of recycled rope but it's not worth the risk even if your car isn't a piece of shit.

At some point my father stopped referring to the station wagon as Brown Beauty and it became 'the car'.

Leaves collected in air vents, a a shopping cart put a ding in a door, and Gus bled out on the back seat on his way to the vet after he was run over by a car. A 40-gallon drum, rescued from the dump to be used as an incinerator, rolled freely side-to-side in the back and ripped a hole in the vinyl. The headliner also ripped when my father took a speed bump too fast while my sister was wearing a plastic tiara. She required several stitches across her forehead and missed a princess-themed birthday party. I called her Herman Munster for a few days until she stabbed me in the shoulder with a fondue fork while I was playing Atari.

"David, I apologize for throwing a used diaper at you. I don't remember doing it but if I did, and urine went in your mouth, I'm honestly sorry. It must have been terrible."

"It was."

"Yes, well, children can be cruel sometimes and I hope you can forgive me. Now, about the kidney transplant, you're the only match and..."

"Remember that time you stabbed me with a fondue fork?"

"No."

"Well you did. While I was playing Atari. I was just a few points away from beating your high score on *Chopper Command*."

The car was stolen a few years later while parked at a cinema complex. It was unusual for my father to go to the movies by himself but apparently he really wanted to see *Rocky IV*. He kept the ticket stub under a magnet on the fridge. The vehicle had a few miles on it by that time. The transmission was shot and the only working dashboard instrument was the check engine light which had a piece of tape over it.

The police rang when they located the car in a creek not far from the cinema. It had been pushed off the road and down a hill, striking a tree at the bottom, and was a write-off. My father agreed with the officer that it was probably kids and did a little fist punch.

"Yes, I blame a lack of discipline. The importance of being a positive role model to your kids can't be stressed enough either. Oh, by the way, I still have my ticket stub from *Rocky IV* if you need to see it. No? Well okay then. Good movie. Definitely worth seeing. He fights a tall Russian guy in this one."

Unlike his love for Brown Beauty, my father's hatred of crows never diminished. The two-inch bald patch on his head was a daily reminder. He purchased a can of spray-on hair that he saw advertised on television but it didn't really look like hair unless you blurred your eyes or he darted back and forth. I'm sure there's been major advances in hair-in-a-can technologies since then though. Don't let my limited experience with the product put you off trying it.

For the rest of his life, my father referred to crows as "black arseholes" and pointed them out with distain wherever we went. Once, while we were at a local swimming center, a couple of crows landed on the lawn near where we sitting on our towels and my father shouted, "Get out of here you black arseholes!"
There was a black family of five sitting behind us and when my father realized, he turned to them and said, "I didn't mean you."
Fired up, the mother of the black family slapped my father with a wet towel hard enough to leave a welt across his back. It must have hurt a lot because it was only the

second time I'd ever heard him scream. There was a bit of a tussle over the wet towel and a toddler got kicked by accident.

We had season tickets so even though we were banned from the swimming center, we kept going. It was around the time my father shaved his sideburns off so he wasn't immediately recognizable. My mother wore a scarf and sunglasses and my sister and I rolled our beach towels into Arab hats and wore them in.

Beach Towel Arab Hats
A step by step guide.

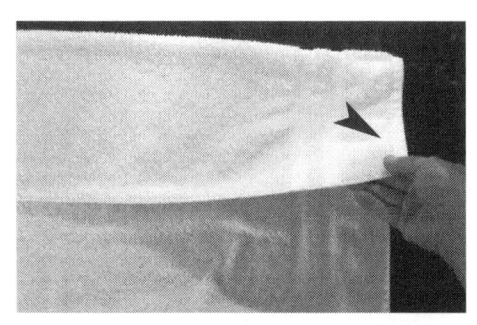

Step 1.

Lay a towel flat. For this example, we have used a white towel but feel free to use a colored or patterned one. Fold a third of the towel over and lay flat.

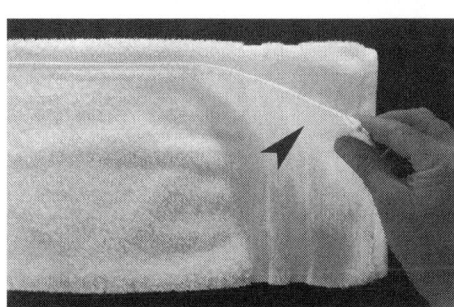

Step 2.

Take the bottom of the towel and fold up. Lay flat. If the top fold doesn't meet the top of the first fold, as in this example, repeat step 1 but don't fold it down so far.

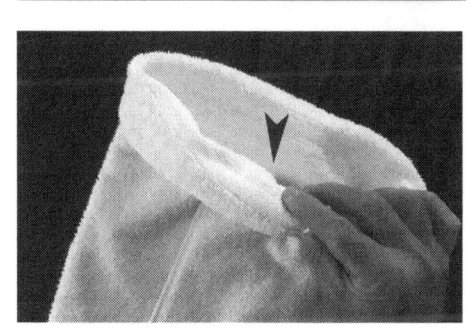

Step 3.

Roll over the end. This can be tricky and you may need to hold the towel against your leg while you roll it or it could come apart and you will have to start again.

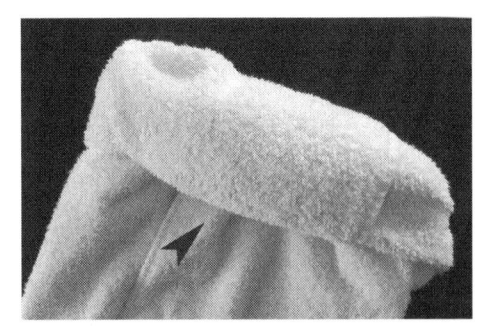

Step 4.

Keep rolling the end over on itself until you have a solid loop. Don't roll too many times or the loop will sit too high on your head. Four rolls should be adequate.

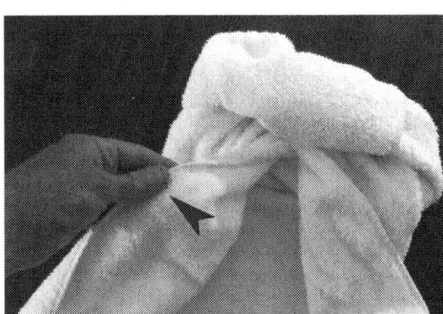

Step 5.

Locate the two flaps and pull them to the side. This will be the front of your Beach Towel Arab Hat.

Step 6.

Place on head. Your Beach Towel Arab Hat is ready for the beach, swimming center or sporting event. It's sun smart and looks great!

For more exciting images of Beach Towel Arab Hats, visit:
www.beachtowelarabhats.com

Buy your own television, Derek

I'm not close friends with Derek. He's a friend of a friend on Facebook and I think they're only friends because Derek's sister repairs rips in vinyl for a reasonable price. All I really know about Derek is that he fixes washing machines for a living and has a perfectly round goatee. It looks like a hairy bagel until he opens his mouth, then it looks like a hairy bagel with severe periodontal disease.

I visited Derek's house once. A small group of us sat in the dark watching the movie *Braveheart* while Derek declared, "Oooh, this is a good bit, watch this bit" every two minutes. It wasn't what I was expecting when someone had stated, "Let's drop in to Derek's house, it's on the way and he's having a party."

On a party hosting scale of 1 to 16, pausing the battle scene in *Braveheart* eighty-six times because you read on the Internet that an extra's wristwatch is visible for a fraction of a second, barely rates a 2. If it wasn't for the fact that a previous employer once made me attend an Enjo Cleaning Products party at his apartment, the score would be lower.

From: Derek Russell
Date: Tuesday 5 June 2018 2.26pm
To: David Thorne and 26 others
Subject: GoFundMe

Hello all,

As you may have heard, our TV died Monday night.

It's no longer under warranty and will cost more to fix than replace. I shopped around and the best price I could find for a replacement is $799.99. It's the same size Sony but a newer model because they don't make ours anymore.

This isn't in our budget at the moment so I have set up a GoFundMe page to help with some of the cost.

Any contribution you can make is appreciated and you're welcome to come over and watch it whenever you like.

The link is:

<Link removed because fuck you, Derek>

Thank you, Derek

From: David Thorne
Date: Tuesday 5 June 2018 2.40pm
To: Derek Russell
Subject: Re: GoFundMe

Dear Derek,

I'm sorry to hear about your television set and understand the need for immediate replacement. *Braveheart* night at Derek's house won't be the same if it's just sitting around staring at the wall while you rattle a tin cup at people.

Although you own several other television sets and GoFundMe campaigns are generally created to raise money for education and medical expenses - not page 4 of the latest Best Buy catalogue - I'm happy to help.

GoFundMe won't accept amounts below $5 so I'll give you the money the next time I see you - possibly standing at an intersection holding a cardboard sign that reads, "New dining room suite and Jacuzzi tub needed."

Regards, David.

From: Derek Russell
Date: Tuesday 5 June 2018 2.52pm
To: David Thorne
Subject: Re: Re: GoFundMe

You're not the boss of GoFundMe campaigns. I'm allowed to raise money for whatever the fuck I want.

And for your information, we have 1 TV, not several. The Vizio in the study was stolen and the Samsung in the dining room won't fit on the Sony mount in the family room. It's a completely different kind of mount.

Derek

From: David Thorne
Date: Tuesday 5 June 2018 3.43pm
To: Derek Russell
Subject: Re: Re: Re: GoFundMe

Derek,

I'm having a similar problem with the suction-cap phone mount in my car; my new phone doesn't fit and I can't afford a new vehicle so I just leave my phone at home now. I should probably just get a landline, we already have the plugs in our walls. As an interim measure, have you considered mirrors?

Placed at the right angle in several locations throughout the home, you'll be able to view the dining room television set from the family room. It will also give you plenty of warning of burglars. They may have taken your Vizio but they will never take your Samsung.

Regardless, I do accept you have the right to solicit money through GoFundMe for whatever purposes you choose. My astonishment at your audacity veered towards abashment and, as way of an apology, I have contributed $25.00 to your campaign. It might not show up right away because I'm on a slow Internet connection.

In return, I ask only that you also donate to the GoFundMe campaign I have just set up:

https://www.gofundme.com/jkwmah-buy-me-a-boat

The money raised will be used to buy me a boat. It needs to have a bed and a bathroom because I'd like to be able to sleep on it. This will save me having to set up a GoFundMe campaign to buy a lake house to stay in when I use the boat.

As way of incentive, if you contribute $25 or more, you'll receive a photo of me on my new boat. Contributing $50 or more gets a photo of me on my new boat without a shirt on. Contributions of $100 or more get a personal invitation to the lake to watch me on my new boat from the shore.

Regards, David.

From: Derek Russell
Date: Tuesday 5 June 2018 3.56pm
To: David Thorne
Subject: Re: Re: Re: Re: GoFundMe

This is why nobody likes you. If you don't want to help then don't help. Nobody's forcing you to and nobody asked for your opinion.

Buy your own fucking boat.

From: David Thorne
Date: Tuesday 5 June 2018 4.02pm
To: Derek Russell
Subject: Re: Re: Re: Re: Re: GoFundMe

Buy your own television, Derek.

Regards, David

From: Derek Russell
Date: Tuesday 5 June 2018 4.08pm
To: David Thorne
Subject: Re: Re: Re: Re: Re: Re: GoFundMe

It's hardly the same thing.

From: David Thorne
Date: Tuesday 5 June 2018 4.21pm
To: Derek Russell
Subject: Re: Re: Re: Re: Re: Re: Re: GoFundMe

No, you have a television. I don't have any boats.

I've read that an intrinsic sense of value is gained by saving to purchase something - and that living within your means is a path to financial security - but that won't get me a boat right now. Taking the ongoing costs of slip fees, maintenance, and inflatable tubes into account, I'll probably need to set up some kind of recurring payment system on GoFundMe.

Can I put you down for $15 per week?

That's less than the cost of hosting three *Braveheart* parties and, as a valued ongoing contributor, you'll receive a subscription to *David's Boat* (a monthly newsletter featuring articles, tips, and dot-to-dot puzzles about boats) and a nautically themed blanket.

Regards, David

From: Derek Russell
Date: Tuesday 5 June 2018 4.33pm
To: David Thorne
Subject: Re: Re: Re: Re: Re: Re: Re: Re: GoFundMe

I've removed you from my list and I'm blocking you.

Adidas

From: David Thorne
Date: Tuesday 5 June 2018 4.37pm
To: Derek Russell
Subject: Re: Re: Re: Re: Re: Re: Re: Re: GoFundMe

Derek,

Was that signoff a subtle hint that you're also in the market for a free pair of athletic shoes?

Regards, David

From: Derek Russell
Date: Tuesday 5 June 2018 4.42pm
To: David Thorne
Subject: Re: Re: Re: Re: Re: Re: Re: Re: Re: Re: GoFundMe

*Adios not adidas dipstick. Autocorrect changed it.

From: David Thorne
Date: Tuesday 5 June 2018 4.50pm
To: Derek Russell
Subject: Re: Re: Re: Re: Re: Re: Re: Re: Re: Re: Re: GoFundMe

Derek,

Bon Voyage is the appropriate maritime phrase. As a future boat owner, I've read up on all the terminology. Looking forward to pontooning my aft during the rudder knots this summer.

Regards, 'Captain' dipstick

From: Derek Russell
Date: Tuesday 5 June 2018 4.55pm
To: David Thorne
Subject: Re: Re: Re: Re: Re: Re: Re: Re: Re: Re: Re: GoFundMe

Looking forward to hearing you drowned.

From: David Thorne
Date: Tuesday 5 June 2018 4.58pm
To: Derek Russell
Subject: Re: Re: Re: Re: Re: Re: Re: Re: Re: Re: Re: Re: Re: GoFundMe

Derek,

I'm capable of keeping my head above water - without imploring others to throw me a swim-noodle.

Regards, David

From: Derek Russell
Date: Tuesday 5 June 2018 5.06pm
To: David Thorne
Subject: Re: Re: Re: Re: Re: Re: Re: Re: Re: Re: Re: Re: Re: Re: GoFundMe

Blocked.

Dot-to-Dot

Answer: It's a boat.

Socks

A hint of first light filtered through dusty blinds. Heather yawned and stretched under the warm duvet, reaching for Hank beside her. Hank snorted and rolled over in his sleep. She smiled and snuggled into him, kissed his neck softly and whispered, "I love you, sleepyhead."

She'd gotten a little tipsy the night before, the three boxes of wine and twelve-pack of Keystone Light had gone straight to her head. She didn't blame the alcohol though, she'd wanted it to happen. They'd wrestled playfully on the couch and she'd kissed him during Double Jeopardy. It was a tentative first kiss. The second kiss was long and wet and had a lot of tongue. Heather wore her Wonder Woman costume to bed, Hank wore socks.

She'd have to tell Ian of course. He was in Ohio, delivering airplane armrests for the company he worked for, but he'd be back the next day. As long as he didn't make things weird, he could move into the spare room until he found another place to live.

Throwing back the duvet, Heather climbed out of bed and made her way downstairs to fix breakfast. Hank heard his food bowl being filled and ran downstairs excitedly to join her.

Spencer's Head Pasted Onto Normal Sized Humans

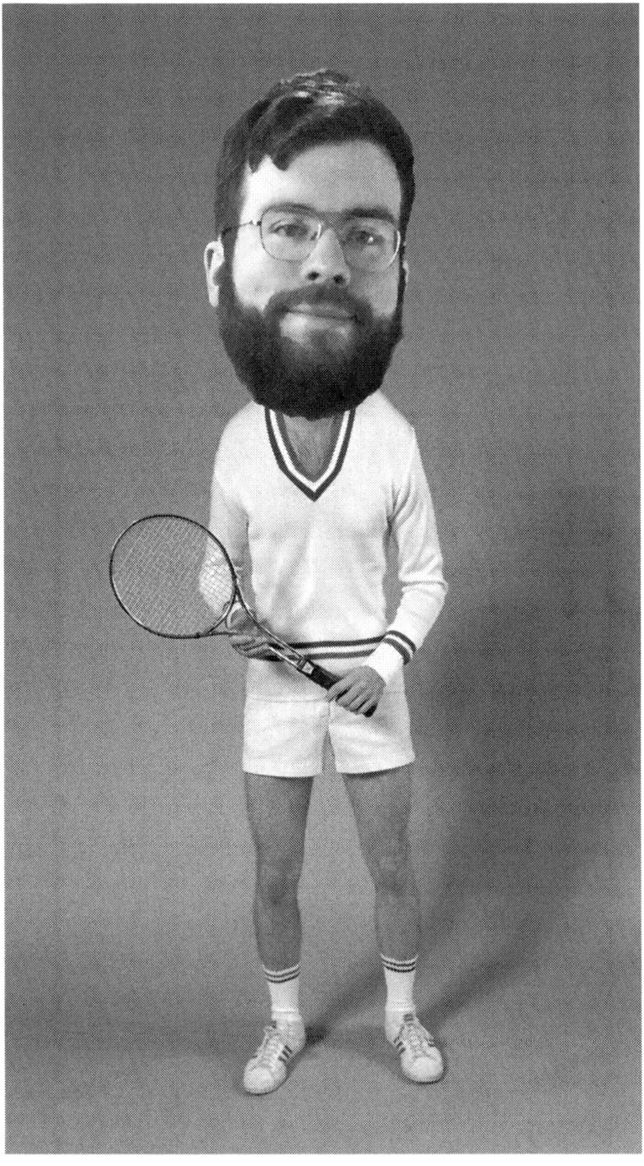

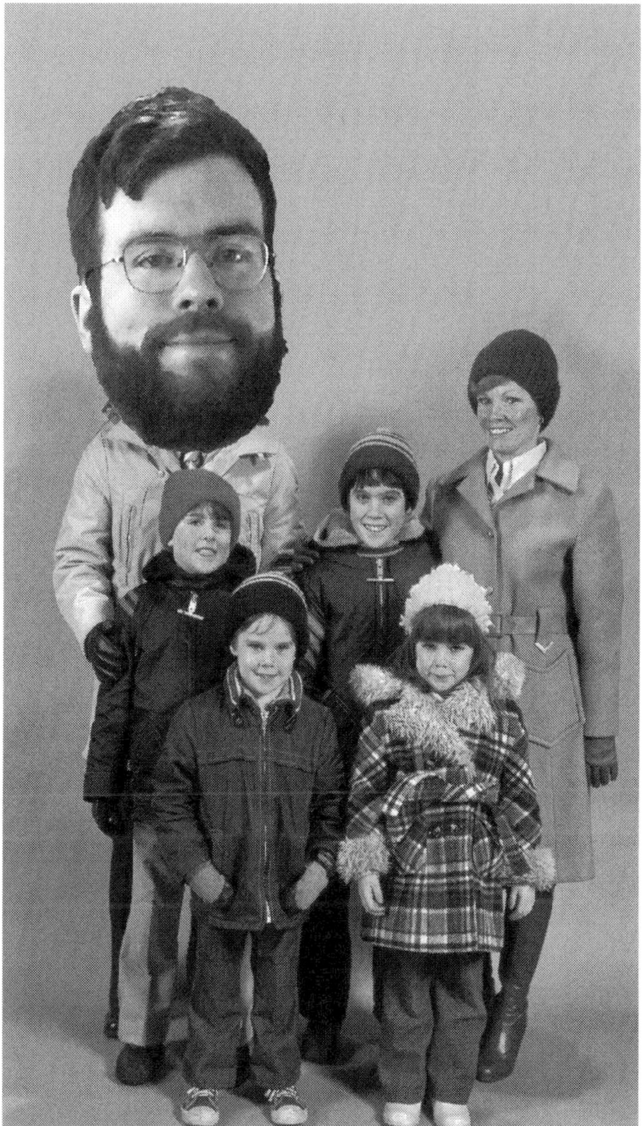

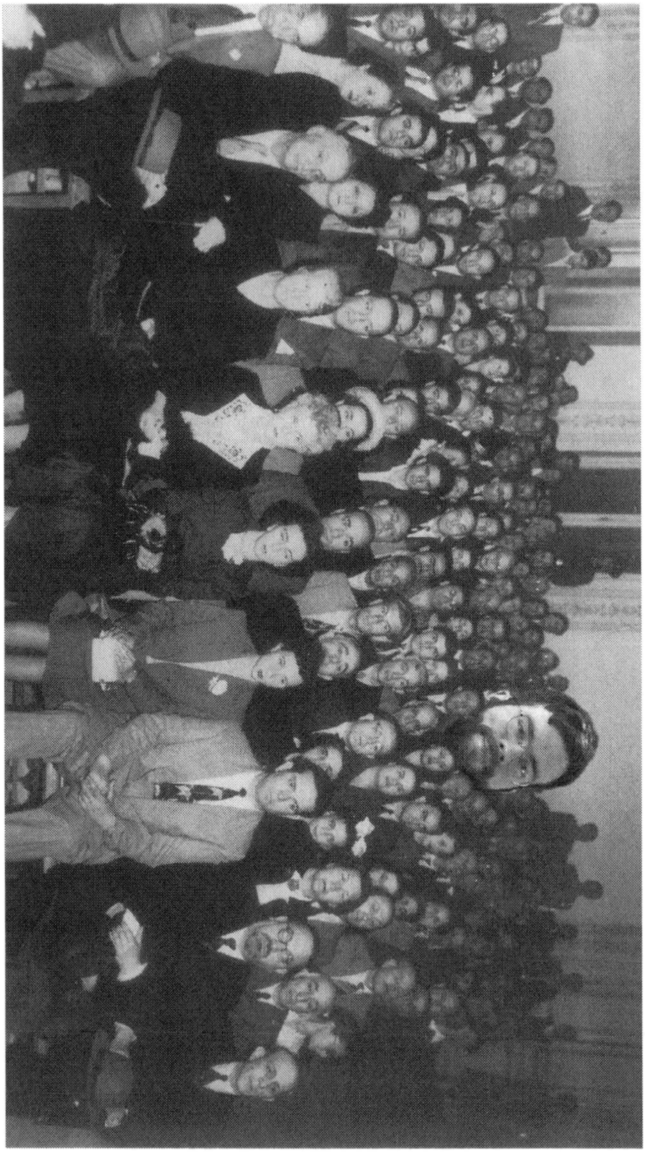

Crowsonly.com

Roadkilllover69

Member since:
03.07.2018

Height:
13"

Genus:
Corvus brachyrhynchos

Occupation:
Crow

Interested in:
Crows

Status:
It's complicated

Smoke:
No

Drink:
Just water

About Me

I'm just your average crow with an encephalization quotient equal to that of many non-human primates. I like to hang out or grab something to eat with friends.

Perfect Date

August 22nd 2017, I found a whole cow in a ditch.

Hobbies

Flying, cawing, building collider accelerators and accelerating two beams of protons to an energy of 6.5 TeV which causes them to collide head-on creating center-of-mass energies of 13 TeV, annoying farmers.

Favorite Music

EDM

Machete Reef

Machete Island

Papua New Guinea

Machetetown

Port Machete

Macheteborough

Machete River

Machete Bay

Machete City

Macheteopolis

Macheteville

Macheteburg

Papua New Guinea

Papua New Guinea is a sparsely populated tropical country, about the same size as Turkmenistan, a hundred or so miles from Australia's northernmost tip of Queensland. It's been said that during low tide you could wade from Australia to Papua New Guinea but you'd have to be a pretty quick wader to make it there before the tide came back in so it's a stupid thing to say. I could probably wade two hundred feet before my legs got tired and I never go deeper than my knees. I've heard that sharks can still attack you in water that shallow but I'd rather be bitten on a knee than the stomach or groin. A few years back, a guy I knew in Adelaide waded out waist deep to retrieve a poorly thrown Frisbee and a shark tore off his left buttock. He survived but he has to use a little half-seat cushion to sit without leaning.

I wouldn't even go knee deep in Queensland, the water there is approximately 20% crocodile. They're salt-water crocodiles so essentially sharks with legs. I read about a woman whose poodle was taken by a salt-water crocodile while she was walking it along the beach. They were several feet from the shoreline but the crocodile exploded out of the water and closed the distance in a fraction of a second. It was a relatively small crocodile, only seven or eight feet, but even the babies can do some damage. To her credit, the woman refused to let go of the leash even after the poodle was ripped in half. She ended up with the head and front half so technically she won the tug'o'war but it wasn't much of a prize. I probably would have let the crocodile have it at that stage. Less to clean up.

If you *were* inclined to wade to Papua New Guinea, you'd need to be a sprint-wader *and* adept at fighting off saltwater crocodiles. You'd also need enough energy left over once you got there to outrun the tribes-people with machetes. Machete is the official language of Papua New Guinea. Screaming as you're hacked to death with a machete is the official second language.

As far as vacation activities go, being hacked to death with a machete isn't most people's first choice and, as such, Papua New Guinea's tourism industry is pretty much nonexistent. I'd rather visit Yemen or West Virginia than Papua New Guinea and I have no desire to hang around with angry bearded men wearing suit jackets in rubble *or* be Billy-Ray's shipping container sex slave.

My friend JM is from West Virginia and while he's generally quite personable, you do occasionally see a hint of the shipping container thing peeking through the thin veneer. Once, while we were camping, he told me that he had a pig when he was young and when I asked if it was his girlfriend, he replied, "You do realize nobody knows you're out here with me, don't you?"

I laughed but JM didn't even smile. He just spat out his tobacco and went to bed so I must have touched a raw nerve. Love is love though; I'm not one to judge. When I was eight, I had a relationship with one of my sister's dolls. It was a four-foot tall, anatomically correct, Snow White doll that looked a lot like a girl at my school named Emma Jenkins. I never had sex with the doll but I kissed it a lot and told it that I loved it. I did almost consummate the relationship one afternoon, when my parents took my sister to a soccer match, but the other team forfeited and my parents returned early to discover us naked in bed. I never saw Snow White again and I had to have 'the talk' that evening. My mother also borrowed a book from the library titled *What's Happening to Me? An Illustrated Guide to Puberty* and left it in my room with a sticky-note that said, "You're normal."

I've only ever met one person from Yemen, he owned a local falafel shop until he was arrested for riding a scooter drunk and deported for being in the country illegally. He's probably standing in rubble wearing a suit jacket right now, waving a AK47 in the air and yelling, "Wolololololol" for no apparent reason. I realize that's a bit stereotypical but if your country condones burying women up to their necks and throwing rocks at their heads for reading, you deserve to cop a bit of flak.

I'm sorry your government and infrastructure is a mess, and that you're at war because your invisible sky wizard says it's okay to eat goat testicles and someone else's invisible sky wizard says it's not, but yelling, "Wolololololol" isn't going to fix anything. Sort it out, dickheads. I realize 'sort it out, dickheads' isn't exactly groundbreaking foreign policy but honestly, if you've got time to stand around in rubble yelling, "Wolololololol", you've got time to sweep up a bit. The ones that ride around in the back of a pickup truck yelling, "Wolololololol" with fifteen other idiots aren't much better but at least they're going somewhere. Hopefully to Home Depot* to buy a few brooms and construction strength garbage bags.

"Will that be all today?"
"Yes, just the brooms and construction strength garbage bags thank you. Oh, and this roll of Mentos. I haven't tried the green apple ones."
"Doing a bit of yard work this weekend?"
"Yes, I've got quite a bit of rubble to clean up. I tried standing on top of it and waving my gun about while yelling wolololololol but it didn't accomplish much."
"No? Well you have a nice day and death to America."
"Same to you. Allahu akbar."

---

* *It's unlikely Yemen has a Home Depot but if I'd written 'Mud Hut Market', nobody would have known what I was talking about.*

Holly makes me rake the gravel in our driveway if it gets a few bumps in it. She's a little overly house-proud though. This autumn, she spent four-hundred-dollars on pumpkins for the front porch just so people driving past can say, "Fuck that's a lot of pumpkins."

"How much did you actually spend on pumpkins, Holly?"
"Not much."
"What are they, like a dollar each?"
"Something like that."
"So about four-hundred dollars then?"
"There's not that many."
"Where did you even find this many pumpkins?"
"I went to a farm."
"What?"
"A pumpkin farm."
"Were they selling them from a cart out the front?"
"No, I picked them."
"Did the farmer see you?"
"Yes, you pay him to pick them. He gives you a cart and a pair of stalk cutters and you walk around and pick the ones you like. It's not a thing in Australia?"
"No. People generally just buy one pumpkin at a time. From a supermarket. If they're making a soup or something."
"You don't decorate your porch in fall?"
"No."
"Well that's just sad."
"Not particularly. You don't think it's weird stacking four-

hundred pumpkins on a porch?"
"It's festive."
"It's a bit over the top."
"No it isn't. I actually need a few more to fill in the gaps. And a couple of hay bales."
"How did you even get this many pumpkins home?"
"I rented a truck from Lowe's."

Someone stopped last week because they thought we were selling them. I gave them a pumpkin for their trouble, figuring we had plenty, but Holly noticed there was one missing when she got home. Apparently it was the best pumpkin in the world and her entire display was ruined. As she was pretty cross about it, I denied any knowledge as to the pumpkin's whereabouts and suggested that perhaps someone had stolen it to make a soup. We have one of those Ring Video Doorbell systems installed now. It cost two-hundred-dollars but can you really put a price on being protected from pumpkin bandits?

I work from home a lot and Holly has access to the Ring on her phone while she's at work so, for the first week after it was installed, I received texts from her every few minutes to let me know that, "The mail just came" and, "There's a cat outside."

I've been accused of exaggerating before so here's a complete list of Holly's security updates during the first day:

9.17am "Can you clean the Ring lens please? It's blurry."
9.22am "That's better. Thank you."
9.24am "Stand in the driveway and wave."
9.26am "Did you cut your hair?"
10.16am "Squirrel on the porch!"
10.18am "Never mind, it's gone now."
10.21am "We should trim the bushes in the front yard."
10.26am "UPS delivered a box. What did you order?"
10.42am "We should get a bird-feeder."
10.44am "The mail came."
11.06am "Has the Ring frozen?"
11.08am "Never mind. I just saw a car drive past."
11.28am "There's a cat outside."
11.34am "It's still there."
11.39am "I watched you put a piece of tape over the lens."
11.43am "Can you take it off please?"
1.22pm "I'm serious."
1.43pm "I'm getting really angry."
2.02pm "Thank you."
2.07pm "Can you move that please? Where did you even get a cardboard cutout of Jonah Hill?"

The punishment for stealing a pumpkin in Yemen is having your hand removed. I'm not sure what the punishment in West Virginia is but it probably involves being chased through a forest and a whole lot of whooping'n'hollering. The punishment for stealing a pumpkin in Papua New Guinea is, obviously, being hacked to death by machete.

When I was in fourth or fifth grade, our class had a guest speaker come in to talk to us about Papua New Guinean culture. He bought in a coconut and a machete and chopped the coconut in half to show us how sharp the blade was. He also showed us a documentary called *Mudmen of Papua New Guinea* about a tribe of natives that wear masks made out of mud. For several months afterwards, I had vivid nightmares about mudmen chasing me with machetes. I'll try drawing one of the masks so you can get an idea of how terrifying they were:

Right, well it didn't come out looking quite as terrifying as I remember. It looks more like a really short ghost or a *South Park* character than a clay mask but you'll just have to imagine a black guy with a machete wearing it. He's chasing you through a shopping mall and your feet weigh a ton for some reason. Also, Emma Jenkins is at the shopping mall with John Stamos from *Full House* and they're holding hands.

The guest speaker also told us a story about a Papua New Guinean village leader named Mutengke. Apparently Mutengke had eight wives, which wasn't nearly enough for someone of his stature, so he sent an invitation to a neighboring village for prospective marriage candidates. The invitation stated that it was a great honor to be one of his wives, as his hut was large and waterproof, and that the candidates should arrive at noon the next day for consideration. It also stated that he was expecting a large turnout so candidates should bring their own mats to sit on.

Asking people to bring their own mats is probably the jungle equivalent of telling people to bring a chair to a barbecue. How good can a barbecue be if the host can't organize chairs? I'm not taking a chair anywhere. I'll stay at home with my vast selection of things to sit on if you can't get your act together.

"David, I'm having a barbecue tomorrow if you're free. I'll fire up the grill around noon."
"Do I have to bring anything?"
"No, just a chair."
"Are you having the barbecue in a field?"
"No, it's at my house but apparently we don't own any chairs. Oh, and it's BYO so bring something to drink and whatever you want put on the grill. And a side dish. Potato salad or something."
"So pack as if I'm going camping, got it. Will anything actually be provided?"
"The venue and great company."
"Right, I'll probably just stay home then."

"No, you have to come. I need you to pick up six bags of ice and a full propane bottle on the way. And a patio umbrella from Home Depot, it's going to be sunny.

I specifically tell people not to bring their own chairs when I have a barbecue. I paid a lot of money for our outdoor setting and I don't want anyone's shitty Coleman fold-up camping chairs ruining the layout. Not enough chairs? Stand. No, we're not bringing the dining room chairs outside, they're West Elm. Perhaps you shouldn't have invited your entire extended family of sixteen, Linda. One afternoon in your over-chlorinated pool honestly isn't worth this shit.

The worst barbecue I've ever been to was right after I moved to America. Holly had posted on Facebook that we were in Harrisonburg (a small village of idiots not far from DC) and a friend of hers named Ina, whom Holly hadn't seen since high school, wanted to catch up. The barbecue was at a trailer park called The Meadows and Holly and I argued at the entrance for five minutes about turning around and going home.

"The name is a bit deceptive. The word meadow implies some kind of field vegetated by grass and other non-woody plants, not trucks, Confederate flags and child molestation."
"There's a field over there."
"That's an airport."

"It's still a field."

"Technically, yes. Not somewhere you'd take the family for a picnic though. I'm going home."

"I promised Ina we'd go, so we're going."

"I'm going to be stabbed and you're going to be chained in a shipping container."

"It doesn't look that bad. Look, that trailer has Christmas decorations. With a giant inflatable snowman."

"It's June."

"We're going."

"If you make me, I'm going to sit in the car with the doors locked. I need more emotional preparation for a situation like this. And a different outfit. I'm wearing a t-shirt that says I heart squirrels. I need some kind of thin western shirt with the sleeves cut off. The kind with studs for buttons. And a Pontiac Trans-Am with a gold eagle on the hood."

"You don't like the t-shirt I got you?"

"Yes, I like the t-shirt. Not a big fan of Gildan though."

Unfortunately, Ina saw us and ran out barefooted in bike shorts and a bikini top to guide us to their trailer. I'm not sure where she found a pair of bike shorts in that size but whoever sells them has a social responsibility to stop. We parked next to red Chevy Silverado pickup truck that was lifted so high, the door handles were head height. It had a sticker on the back window that said 'Not My President!' above Obama's face with a red target over it, and a bigger sticker that said Chevrolet. So that people driving behind can tell it's a Chevrolet without having to get too close I suppose.

"What kind of pickup truck is that in front of us?"
"I'm not sure, I'll speed up and check…"
"Just be careful, the roads are icy."
"Oh, wait, it's a Chevrolet. I don't need to drive dangerously because he's got a big sticker on the back window that says Chevrolet. We should get one of those stickers for our Saturn. One that says Saturn obviously, not Chevrolet."
"Yes, we should. You can't put a price on safety."

There were five or six other guests at the barbecue, not including Ina's boyfriend Luke and their four children Tucker, Kyle, Dakota and Hunter. One of the guests, a 400-pound man in his fifties named TNT, had one tooth, no shirt, and two crossed sticks of dynamite tattooed on his chest. I asked him what did and he replied, "Eat pussy."

Two of the guests were Ina's parents. Her father looked like a stick insect wearing a Santa beard and her mother looked like a pudding wearing a wig. They were both deaf so I guess they met at some kind of deaf camp or something. I've got nothing against deaf people but the 'nuhugghnnn' noise gets a bit annoying and there's no point trying to teach me how to say banana with eighty sequential hand movements that look like you're conjuring a water demon because I'm not going to remember it. Just carry a pad and pencil around and either write the word banana or draw one. Also, the jazz fingers instead of clapping thing. Not a huge fan.

I worked with a deaf guy named Neil for a couple of years. He looked like a human/axolotl hybrid and had red hair so there wasn't a lot going for him. We worked in different departments - he was an account rep at Amcor while I worked in the art department - but we often had to drive to attend client meetings together. The trips were excruciating because he drove a manual hatchback and, even at highway speeds, never went above second gear. The engine screamed and the RPM gauge redlined while he sat there oblivious. Sometimes I'd try to alert him to the fact but he'd just smile and nod and say, "Nuhugghnnn." We were late for a meeting one afternoon and, after gunning his vehicle harder than usual, the engine blew up. Cylinders actually punched through the hood and flames came out the air-conditioning vents. Also, if you can't hear people knocking on your office door, perhaps lock it if you're planning on having a lunch wank.

Ina's parents lived in the trailer next door, which was probably quite handy for babysitting and grits & squirrel stew Sundays. Her father invited me over to look at his collection of brown slacks and showed me some kind of special video camera setup on his television for deaf people. I had to sit in a chair and wave at a deaf person in Alaska.

Another guest, a blonde woman wearing a hoodie with *Team Jesus* written across it, told me I talked funny and when I explained I was from Australia, she asked if I'd driven to the United States.

"No, there's actually a fair bit of water between the two countries so you'd need some kind of amphibious vehicle with a decent sized fuel tank to make it by driving."
"What?"
"You'd need an amphibious vehicle."
"What's amphibious mean?"
"Like a frog."
"TNT, this guy says he came to America on a frog."
"No I didn't."
"Have you ever seen a kangaroo?"
"Yes. Thousands."
"Can you ride them?"
"No."
"Have you ever seen an emu?"
"Yes. But it's pronounced 'eem-you' not 'ee-moo'."
"Can you ride eemooyoos?"
"What's your fascination with riding wildlife?"
"I don't have a fascination. Have you ever seen a crocodile?"
"Yes, Queensland beaches are crawling with them. And before you ask, no you can't ride them."
"Why would anyone want to ride a crocodile? Have you ever seen a dingo?"
"Holly, how long are we staying?"

"A few hours."

"Right. Don't forget we've got that thing later. That thing that we have to go to."

"There's no thing."

There were no seats at all outside so we all sat inside the trailer on a damp brown velour lounge suite, staring at each other and listening to a Kid Rock CD. Ina had hand painted the phrase *Live, Laugh, Love* in large script above a pot belly stove and we all agreed that it added value to the trailer and that she was like some kind of reincarnation of Gandhi.

There was also no actual barbecue but Luke had slow-cooked a large pot of bear meat stew for two days. We each had to put in five-dollars for it but, because Holly and I are vegetarian and didn't eat, we received a two-dollar discount. When a bottle of Jim Beam was passed around to swig from - after everyone had finished the beer that Holly and I had bought - we said that we were going to get more beer and drove home instead.

Later we learnt that Luke had driven to buy more alcohol, with two children in the back, and rolled his Chevrolet. He was charged with child endangerment, driving under the influence, driving with a suspended license, and driving an unregistered vehicle. He did ninety days in jail and while he was locked up, Ina slept with his brother and gave TNT a blowjob for twenty-dollars.

I've only ever cheated on someone once in my life. I was eight and I wasn't aware that Morgan Nelson and I were dating when I circled *Yes* on a note that asked *Do you like Emma?* Morgan and I had ridden our bikes part of the way home together the day before so it's possible something was said that I missed or she misinterpreted. Maybe she was just impressed by my bunny-hops. According to relayed monkey-bar intel, Emma didn't actually like me at all. The note had been a test, which I'd failed, and Morgan and Emma were planning to wait for me outside the front school gates after class and beat me up. As Morgan was a bit of a heifer and Emma took Karate lessons, there was a very real possibility of being hurt so I stayed late after class and left through the back gates. The next day, my explanation of staying late to research caterpillars for a school report was declared a weak excuse and I was accused of being too scared to fight girls - which I vehemently denied to the point of declaring I'd fight five girls at once. They were waiting for me at the bike racks after the bell rang, five girls and several spectators, but I was prepared. At lunchtime, I'd emptied out my drinking bottle and filled it with piss.

Noon came and went and nobody showed up for Mutengke's marriage auditions. Outraged by this blatant sign of disrespect, Mutengke sent a group of men to the neighboring village that night to hack their children to death with machetes. I raised my hand at this point in the story to ask the obvious question.

"Yes? The young man in the *Mork & Mindy* t-shirt?"
"Was it because of the mats?"
"Sorry?"
"The mats."
"I'm sorry, I don't understand what you're asking."
"The reason nobody showed up. Was it because Mutengke told them they had to bring their own mats?"
"No, the mats haven't got anything to with the story."
"It was on the invite. To bring mats."
"The mats don't matter."
"Then why didn't they go?"
"Because Mutengke was old and mean and their village was better. It was on a beach."
"Where was Mutengke's village?"
"In the jungle."
"You should have told us all that at the start of the story."
"David, shut up and let Mr Tonkwokoki finish."

A week after the massacre, Mutengke sent another invitation to the neighboring village and twelve women showed up. I assume with their own mats. You can probably tell where this is going.

The women were plump and of childbearing age so Mutengke decided he'd marry them all. To celebrate the upcoming marriages, the village held a feast that night which included copious amounts of tumbuna - a popular local alcoholic beverage made from fermented guava and taro roots.

Mutengke awoke the next morning to a silent village. The children and his prospective brides were gone, the adults had all had their throats cut in their sleep.

A week later, Mutengke, dirty and half-starved, wandered into the neighboring village. Apparently it was a better village that his. On a beach. Rather than being driven away, the villagers gave him a bowl of mumu - a traditional dish of pork and rice - and a mat to sit on at the edge of village. For five days,* Mutengke watched the thriving village go about their daily activities. The people were happy and sang and laughed as they went about their day-to-day activities. He recognized two of his own children amongst the other children taken from his village and the twelve women he had planned to marry. The women laughed and played with the children, hugged them, scolded them when they were naughty and consoled them when there were tears.

On the sixth day, one of the women bought Mutengke his daily bowl of mumu and he asked, "Why did you not kill me that night?"
The woman nodded towards a group of children playing nearby and asked, "Which of those children are yours?"

I assume he just sat on the mat the entire time. The story didn't cover this in detail but I've seen documentaries about tribes and there seems to be a lot of mat sitting. My favorite tribe is the African one that jumps.

Mutengke pointed out his two sons.

"No," the woman corrected him, "Those children are ours. You have nothing. No people, no home. Even the mat you sit on does not belong to you. It was my daughters."

Mutengke lowered his head and stared into his bowl. The meat was tinged green. "This pork is rancid," he said.

"Yes," the woman replied, "It's two weeks old. And it's not pork."

Which is a bit rough. I think everyone in the class, including our teacher, was expecting a positive message, possibly even a happy ending such as Mutengke's sons taking him by the hand and saying, "Come over to the fire with the rest of the family, Father." But no, apparently keeping your enemies alive so you can feed them dead children was the message.

The class was silent for several seconds, then Mr Tonkwokoki yelled and waved about his machete. Several students screamed then giggled nervously, our teacher had a hearty guffaw and pantomimed having a heart attack. I thought it was odd and a bit of a cop out. The story didn't have an ending, just a jump-scare. Like the campfire story about the man with the white face and red eyes that looks in people's windows.

A few plot holes also stood out; firstly, if it was two weeks between when the children were slaughtered and Mutengke arrived at the village, why weren't the dead children already buried? Or did they dig a few back up when he got there? Secondly, why was Mutengke half-starved? Did the women take the village's food supply back with them? There wasn't a pig leg or a couple of coconuts left over from the feast the night before to tide Mutengke over? Also, who sleeps through everyone having their throats cut? I'm no expert but you'd think there'd be a bit of thrashing and bloody gurgling going on and, after slaughtering a bunch of children with machetes, it would seem sensible to keep a few guards posted just in case the neighboring villagers also own machetes.

"Oh no, Mutengke's men have slaughtered our children. Should I tell everyone to grab their machetes?"
"No, give it a week and see if he sends another invitation. If he does, send the mothers of the dead children to steal their children and slaughter the adults while they sleep. Not Mutengke though, dead men feel no loss. Oh, and tell the women to bring back all the food."
"Right. Seems like an overly complicated plan but you're the boss. Should we bury our children in the meantime?"
"No, not yet."

I raised a couple of these plot holes with Mr Tonkwokoki but was told I'd missed the point of the story. Emma Jenkins asked if girls in Papua New Guinea wear grass skirts and was told it was an excellent question.

0.388" x 0.388" Box

Perfect for 0.388" x 0.388" items.
Simply cut along outside line, fold on dotted lines, and glue bottom and side flaps.

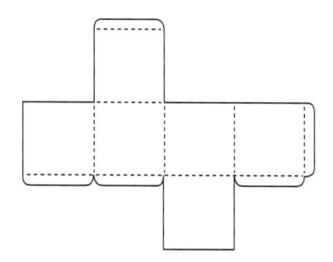

Power Washer 5000

"We should call it the 'Power Washer'."

"That's what it is, Walter. Pressure washers are also known as 'power washers'."

"Bullshit. I've never heard anyone call it a 'power' washer."

"The term 'power washing' is interchangeable with 'pressure washing'; like couch and sofa."

"'Power Washer 5000' then. Because it has 5000 psi of pressures."

"The packaging will include the description '5000psi Pressure Washer'. It's like naming a four slice toaster 'Toaster 4, 4 slice toaster'."

"No, it isn't. What's your suggestion then?"

"I've made a short list but am leaning towards 'Torrent.'"

"Pfft. What's a pressure washer got to do with downloading movies?"

Meetings

There's a lot that could be said about our new account rep Kenneth but none of it is interesting so I'll keep it to one paragraph. I once slept for twenty minutes during one of his meetings and when I awoke, he was explaining the same pie chart that I'd nodded off to. I looked around the boardroom to see if anyone had noticed and two other people were asleep. Melissa, our secretary, actually had her mouth open with a line of spittle running down to the table. I poked a pen in her mouth and she gagged and woke up startled, which I found pretty amusing. I chuckled through the rest of the meeting and for an hour or two afterwards whenever I thought about it. It was the most entertaining thing that has ever happened in one of Kenneth's meetings.

From: Kenneth Warner
Date: Monday 6 August 2018 10.16am
To: David Thorne
Subject: Meeting

David, you missed the meeting this morning. Can we reschedule that for 3pm please?

Ken

From: David Thorne
Date: Monday 6 August 2018 10.22am
To: Kenneth Warner
Subject: Re: Meeting

Kenneth,

Unfortunately, that won't be possible as I've decided I won't be attending any more of your meetings. If boredom could take on physical form and punch people in the face over and over again until they black out, I'd pick that over ten minutes in the boardroom with you.

David

From: Kenneth Warner
Date: Monday 6 August 2018 10.27am
To: David Thorne
Subject: Re: Re: Meeting

David,

I don't give a flying fuck what you'd pick. I've rescheduled the meeting for 3pm and I expect you to be there.

Ken

From: David Thorne
Date: Monday 6 August 2018 10.41am
To: Kenneth Warner
Subject: Auto responder

Thank you for your email.

I'm currently out of the office but will reply to your email upon my return. If you require assistance during my absence, please contact Kenneth. He will be happy to arrange a meeting, as it's all he does. Last week we had fourteen meetings. Seven of which were to discuss where we are on projects, five were to discuss why we are behind on projects, two were to discuss the importance of meeting deadlines, and one was about mouse droppings in the kitchen which turned out to be burnt rice.

Regards, David

From: Kenneth Warner
Date: Monday 6 August 2018 10.50am
To: David Thorne
Subject: Re: Auto responder

I know you're in your office. I saw you close the blinds. There were a total of 9 meetings last week not 14 and you didn't attend 4 of them. We're having a meeting at 3pm. Gary from Emerson is expecting an update on the pressure washer packaging and I need to know where we are with the project. Also, as you are fully aware, I prefer Ken thank you.

Ken

From: David Thorne
Date: Monday 6 August 2018 10.58am
To: Kenneth Warner
Subject: Emerson packaging update

Kenneth,

Packaging is completed pending revised dot-point copy from Ben.

Gary signed off on the name *Torrent 5000* and product decals were approved last week.

You can let him know that he will receive a proof for the packaging by Wednesday.

David

From: Kenneth Warner
Date: Monday 6 August 2018 11.22am
To: David Thorne
Subject: Re: Emerson packaging update

Thank you for the update but I'd still like to have a meeting at 3pm.

Ken

....

From: David Thorne
Date: Monday 6 August 2018 11.43am
To: Kenneth Warner
Subject: Re: Re: Emerson packaging update

Kenneth,

Of course you would. Without a meeting to schedule, attend or preside over, you shrivel like a forgotten carrot at the back of a crisper drawer.

The fact that a two-minute email is more productive than a two-hour meeting doesn't matter. An email doesn't allow you to point at things and repeat what's just been said in an irrelevant and annoying manner or provide you a captive audience for monologue from *Aimless: An Evening with Kenneth*.

We also don't get to find out what everyone did on the weekend, how much Jennifer's bathroom is going to cost to remodel, or why Walter decided to get his hair cut a little shorter this time.

I understand you get bored but have you considered taking up a hobby? You're like an old lady who walks to the post office each day to buy a single stamp so she has someone to talk to about her cat that died in 1947.

I have two projects to be completed today and you're up to date with the Emerson packaging, so what exactly is the point of having another meeting?

David

From: David Thorne
Date: Monday 6 August 2018 12.07pm
To: Kenneth Warner
Subject: Update

Kenneth,

Also, just in case the 3pm meeting *is* to discuss weekend activities, bathrooms and haircuts, I've emailed everyone and am only waiting on Mike, Sarah, and you to respond:

Melissa spent the weekend cleaning because her parents are visiting Thursday. It's their anniversary and she's going to cook them dinner.

Ben played PUBG for 48 hours straight and apparently had a chicken dinner.

Jodie went out Saturday night and spent Sunday recovering on the couch binge-watching *The Ozark* on Netflix.

Jennifer went shopping with her husband for granite counter tops for her bathroom renovation but they decided to go with quartz.

Walter replied, "Not much, you?"

Apparently Jennifer's bathroom is going to cost fifteen thousand dollars to remodel because she wants heated floor tiles. Walter was thinking of letting his hair grow out but decided it's easier to do when it's short.

David

From: Kenneth Warner
Date: Monday 6 August 2018 12.50pm
To: David Thorne
Subject: Re: Update

It's none of your business what I did on the weekend and I don't appreciate being called a carrot or an old lady. The meeting at 3pm is to discuss why the Emerson project ran over schedule by 3 weeks. By working out what went wrong, we can prevent this happening in the future.

Just so you know, I intend to have a meeting with Mike and Jennifer to discuss your attitude and why you continually try to make my job harder.

Ken

....

From: David Thorne
Date: Monday 6 August 2018 1.13pm
To: Kenneth Warner
Subject: Re: Re: Update

Kenneth,

Nobody is trying to make your job harder. We all realize you have a heavy schedule of chair swiveling, ceiling watching and pen tapping to get through between meetings. Those mines aren't going to sweep themselves and online quizzes about what kind of donut you are won't be accurate unless you take the time to think about and answer each question honestly. We can't all be pink icing with sprinkles, Kenneth, someone has to be the plain donut.

I assumed the reason for the Emerson packaging not meeting deadline was obvious but I've attached a breakdown in pie chart format to help visualization.

David

☐ Product naming, design, development, application, packaging and copy.

■ Kenneth's fucking meetings.

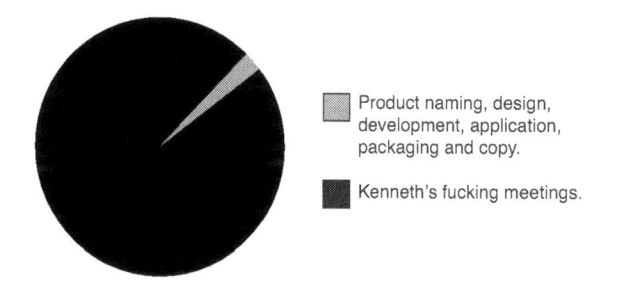

From: Kenneth Warner
Date: Monday 6 August 2018 1.39pm
To: David Thorne
Subject: Re: Re: Re: Update

I've printed out your emails and will be speaking to Jennifer and Mike about this. Quite frankly, I've had enough of you and your whole fucking department.

Ken

F26-A

Date	8 / 6 / 2018	Date of offence	8 . 6 . 2018

Name of person filing F26-A: Ken Warner

Name/s of person/s involved: David Thorne

Complaint type: [X] Internal [ ] External [ ] Other:

Description: Ref: [X] Formal [ ] Med [ ] Class 1 [ ] Class 2

Personal insults. Refusal to attend meetings.

Belittled my position. Stated I was irrelevant, annoying and aimless.

Said he would rather be punched in the head by boredom taking on physical form than spend 10 minutes in the boardroom with me.

Accused me of playing games and taking online quizzes instead of working.

Called me a shrivelled carrot and an old lady buying stamps.

Called me a plain donut.

Action Requested: [X] Disciplinary [ ] Mediation [ ] Other:

Signature: K. Warner   8 / 6 / 2018

Office Use Only

RECEIVED AUG 06 2018

Ref: [X] F26-A [ ] F26-B   Lodged: [ ] Y [ ] N

F26-B Attached [ ] Y [X] N   Date: AUG 06 2018

From: Jennifer Haines
Date: Monday 6 August 2018 2.27pm
To: David Thorne **CC:** Kenneth Warner
Subject: F26-A

David, I'm cc'ing Ken on this email.

Please make yourself available for meetings. Communication between departments allows both parties to perform their job to the best of their abilities. Personal insults are not permissible in the workplace.

Rather than lodge the complaint, I'd prefer we all met to discuss the issue like adults. Will 4pm today work for you?

Thank you, Jennifer

From: David Thorne
Date: Monday 6 August 2018 2.35pm
To: Jennifer Haines **CC.** Kenneth Warner
Subject: Re: F26-A

Jennifer,

I'd rather you just lodged the complaint to be honest. I'm sure Ken has a fractal boner over the prospect of a meeting to discuss missed meetings but I actually have real work to get done. I will apologize to him for the insults.

David

From: David Thorne
Date: Monday 6 August 2018 2.48pm
To: Kenneth Warner
Subject: Apology

Kenneth,

I'm sorry for calling you a plain donut, a shriveled carrot, and an old woman buying stamps.

The comparisons were uncalled for, fitting and hurtful. I also apologize for belittling your role at this company. I do understand how important your meetings are to you and my limited ability to pretend they don't suck the life force out of everybody in the room is something I need to personally work on.

David

From: Kenneth Warner
Date: Monday 6 August 2018 3.07pm
To: David Thorne
Subject: Re: Apology

Apology not accepted.

Mess with the bull, you get the horns.

Ken

Meetings (Update)

From: David Thorne
Date: Friday 10 August 2018 2.06pm
To: Kenneth Warner
Subject: Emerson contract proof

Kenneth,

Emerson packaging proof was signed off on Wednesday. I have the cromolyn (contract proof) in my office if you'd like to see it.

David

From: Kenneth Warner
Date: Friday 10 August 2018 2.17pm
To: David Thorne
Subject: Re: Emerson contract proof

Oh you'd like to have a meeting in your office would you? I'm afraid I can't because your meetings are boring. I'd rather be punched by boredom coming to life than spend 10 minutes in your office.

Ken

Butterfly Knife

"Seb, there's a package here for you. What did you buy?"
"A butterfly knife."
"Really?"
"Yes."
"Are you in a gang?"
"No. I just wanted one."
"Why?"
"You can't get them in Australia. They're banned."
"There's probably a reason for that. What are you going to do with it?"
"Twirl it."
"What for?"
"You give it a twirl and it opens and then you give it another twirl and it shuts. It's clever."
"Is it though?"
"You're only saying that because you don't have the skillset."
"It's twirling a knife. That's one step away from twirling a baton."
"No it isn't. It's very masculine. Soldiers do it."

David & His Best Friends Being Sun Safe at the Beach

> Thanks for making us Beach Towel Arab Hats, David.

> You're welcome, cats.

They're sun safe and fashionable. Plus it means we don't have to carry our towels.
Yes, they're very convenient.

We're basically just filler at this point, aren't we.
Pretty much.

I figured. There's only so much you can really say about Beach Towel Arab Hats. Also, just so you know, they're only partly sun safe because of the hole in the top.
That provides ventilation. Otherwise your head might sweat.
Valid point.

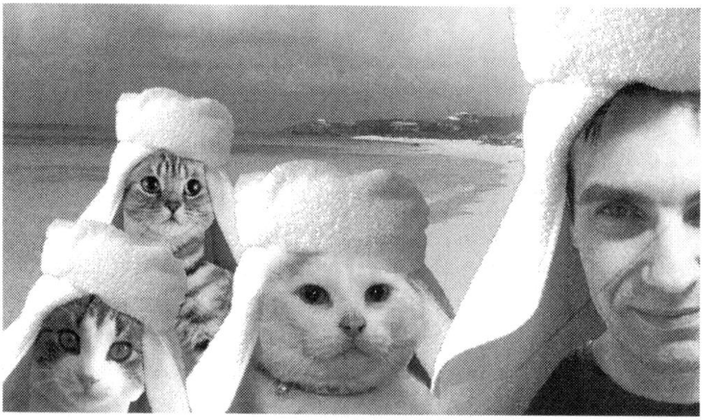

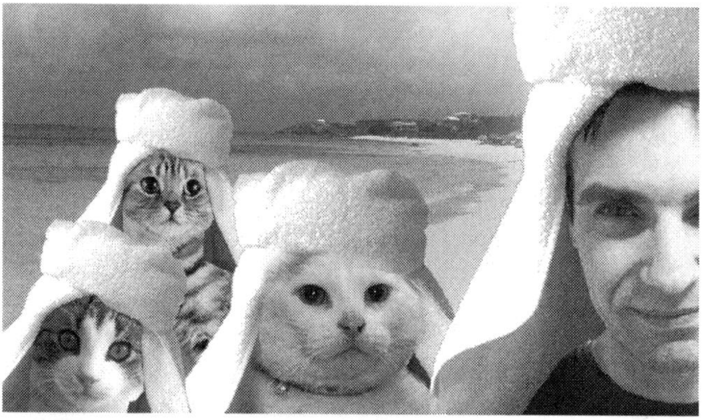

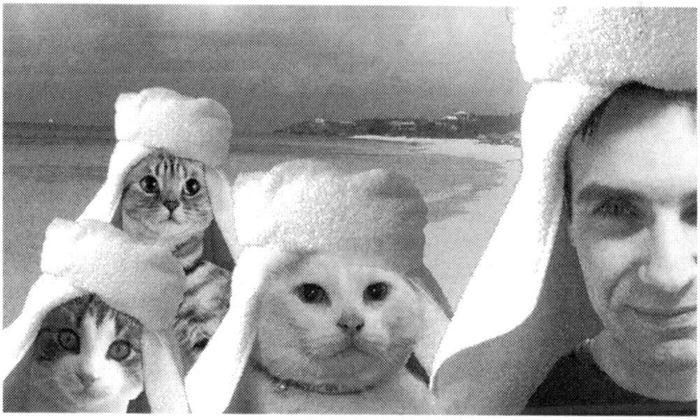

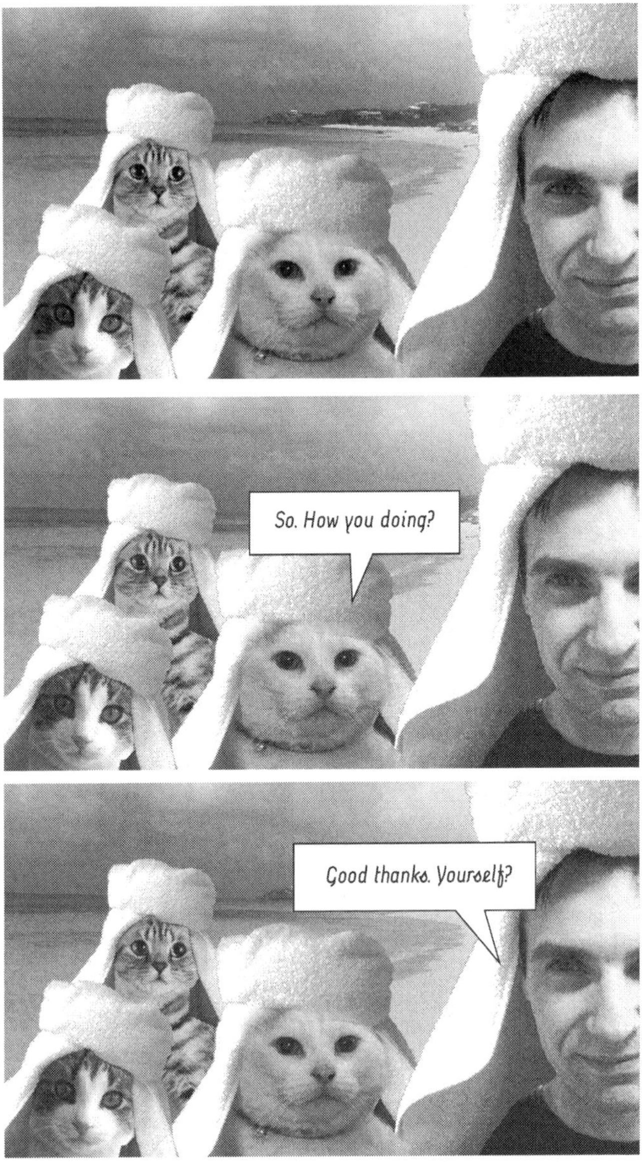
So. How you doing?
Good thanks. Yourself?

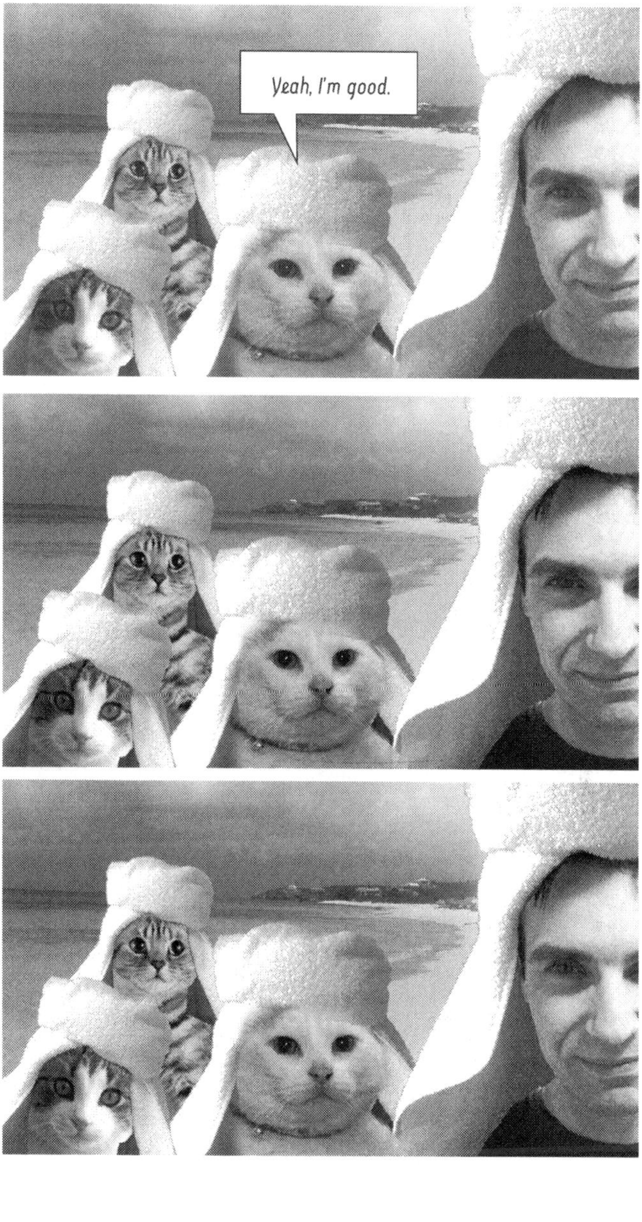
Yeah, I'm good.

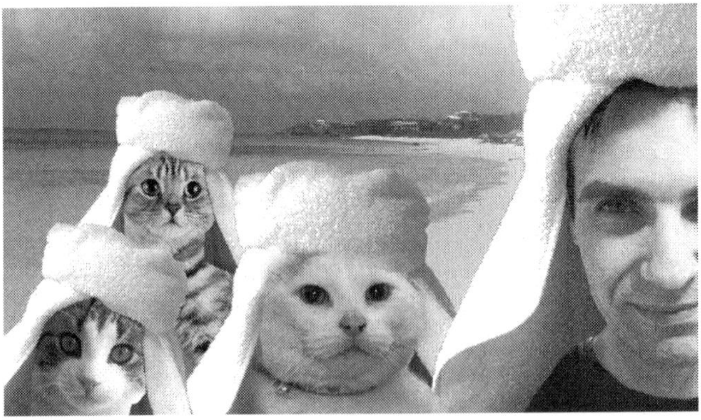

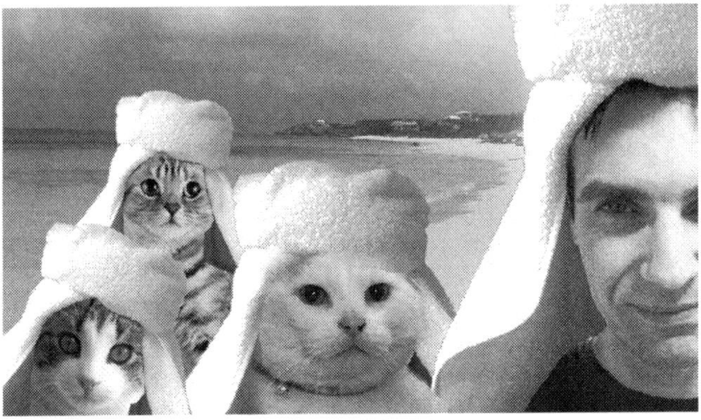

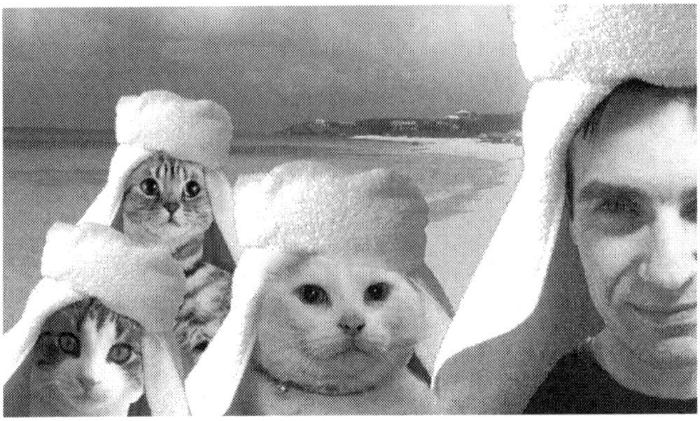

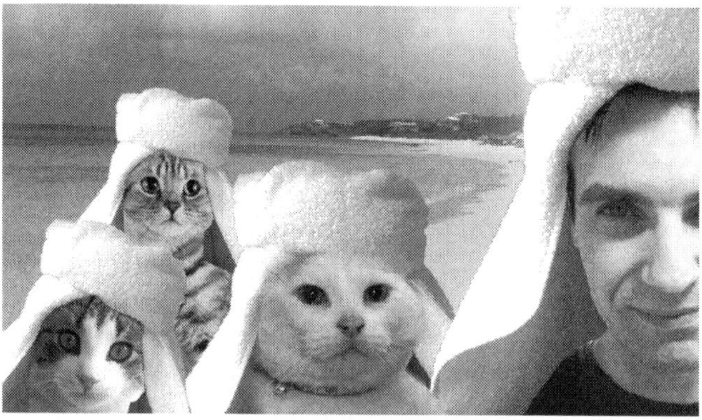

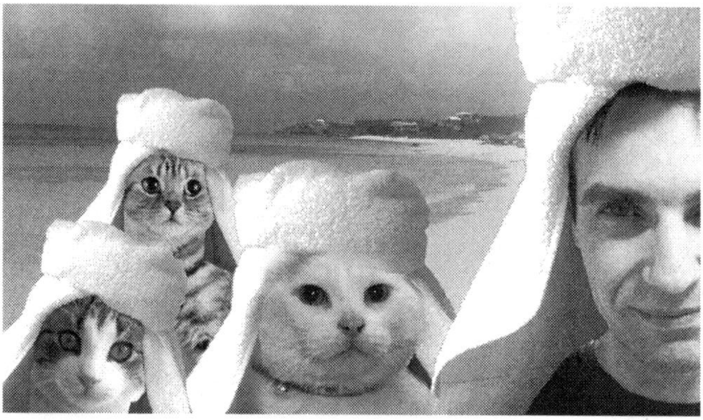

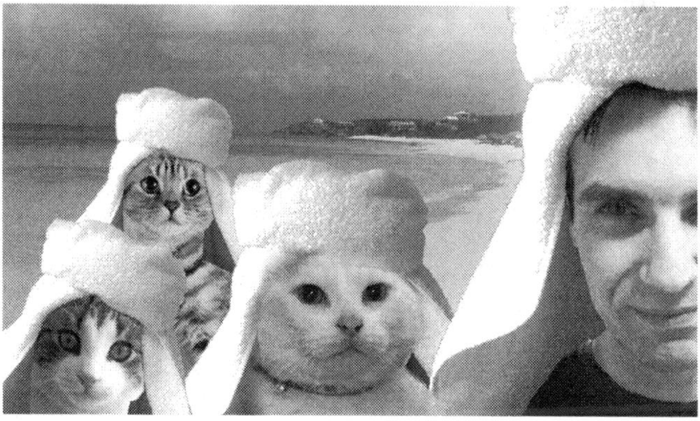

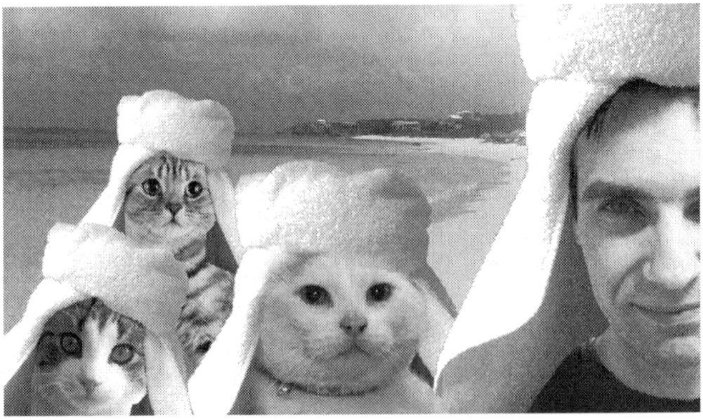

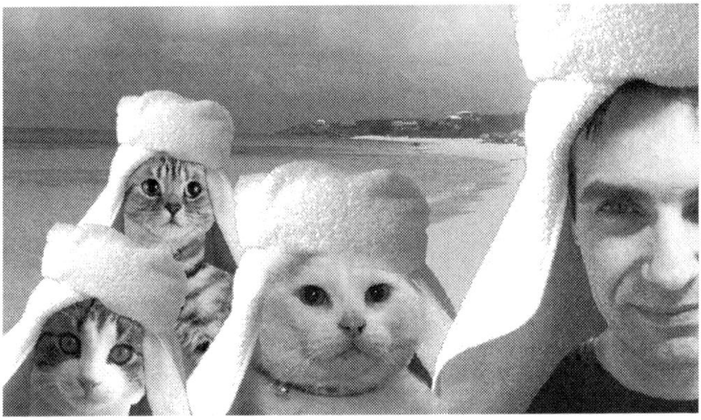

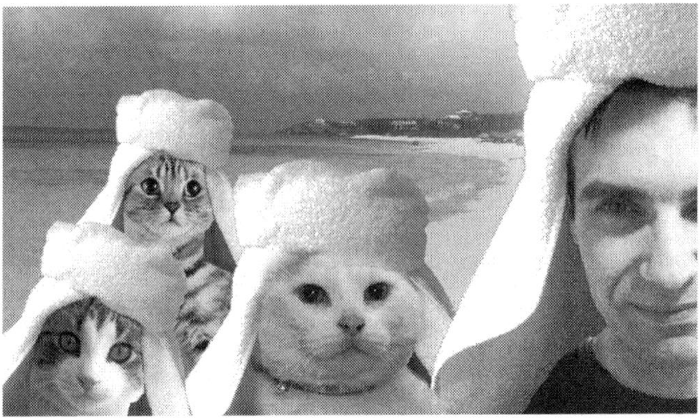

It just keeps going.

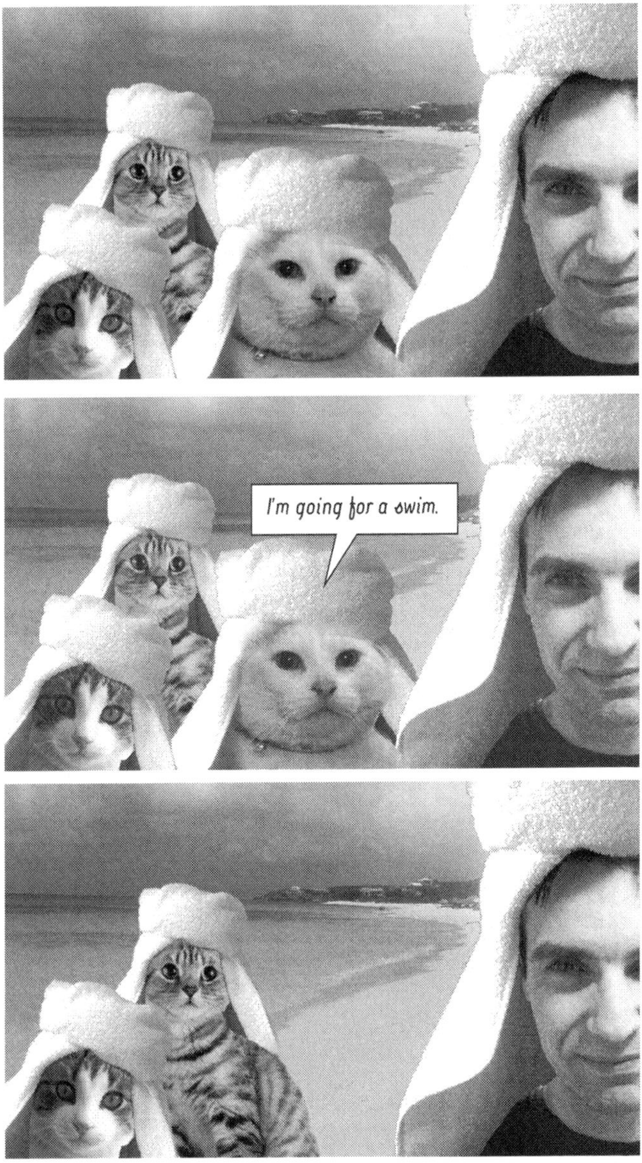
I'm going for a swim.

Boats

"It's getting warm outside," the Lowe's cashier declared. She scanned a spray can of Flex Seal and put it in a plastic bag, "It will be summer before we know it."
For some reason, I decided the word *indubitably* was an appropriate response but, as I said it, my brain had a mini-stroke and it came out as "Indo bibly bibly."
The cashier stared at me strangely and I decided my only recourse was to pretend I speak another language so I added, "Bibly albib oobibly."
Remembering a word from French lessons at school, I also threw in "la pomme" to make my new language believable, which I think means apple.

For those not familiar with Flex Seal, it's basically a can of liquid rubber that you spray on things to seal them. In the product advertisement, a chubby excited guy named Phil drills holes in the bottom of a boat, seals the holes with the product, then goes for a boat ride. It's like a thirty-second episode of *MacGyver*. What they don't tell you in the commercial is that the product is highly flammable. It probably states it on the can somewhere but who reads labels? I once chased a bee around the house for twenty minutes with a can of Pam cooking spray because the can is the same shape and color as Raid.

The bee just wouldn't die so I ended up whipping it out of the air with a towel. It was a pretty impressive shot and a tragedy that nobody else was home to witness it. We have floorboards throughout the house and they were fairly slippery from the Pam for a few days. The stairs were the worst, especially if you were wearing socks. Holly slipped while carrying a coffee and there are still splashes on the ceiling and a head shaped dent in the wall. She accused me of attempted murder, which I found rather insulting as I'm capable of coming up with a much better plan than slippery steps. Also, where I'd sprayed the walls, the paint absorbed the oil and turned a shade darker. There are eight wiggly lines in the living room and two large spots in the hallway where the bee rested for a moment and I attempted to drown it. A week later, I sprayed a Pyrex oven dish with Raid so it's obviously too easy to mix up the products. Seb said it was the best frittata he's ever had and he didn't die so maybe there's something in that.

"Will that be all for you today sir?"
"Bibly."
"Your total is $12.98, do you have a Lowe's card?"
"Bib."
"Credit or debit?"
"Bebit."
"Would you like the receipt in the bag?"
"Bibly."
"Have a nice day."
"Bib boo."

I'm not sure what the point of a cashier asking, "Will that be all for you today?" is. I'm hardly going to take a cordless screwdriver out of my jacket and say, "No, this as well." It's just as pointless asking, "Did you find everything you were looking for?" They ask that at TJ Maxx and nobody goes to TJ Maxx looking for something in particular. You just wander around aimlessly and eventually end up at the checkout with an armful of soaps, two oddly shaped t-shirts that you'll throw away when you get home, four candles, a bottle of olive oil with a sprig of rosemary in it, and a ceramic owl.

"Did you find everything you were looking for today?"
"No, do you have two brass shelf brackets shaped like monkeys? I saw them on West Elm but there's no way I'm paying two hundred dollars."

Three weeks prior to my visit to Lowe's to purchase Flex Seal, Holly and I bought a boat. We'd talked about buying a boat several times over the years as we live an easy drive to Virginia's Smith Mountain Lake and have rented houseboats on it several times. We invited our friends JM and Lori to join us once but they're not allowed to come again because while I was relaxing in the water in a tube, JM sat on the back of the houseboat and read out Republican propaganda likening people who want Confederate statues torn down to ISIS members. The article was written by my dentist for a local paper so I had to change dentists after that.

I understand the whole *It's heritage not hate* rhetoric but I'd prefer to have my teeth checked by someone more focused on family dental care than clan membership drives.

"The Civil War wasn't about slavery, it was about government overreach. It's also important to keep in mind that the Confederate Battle Flag was simply just that. A battle flag. It wasn't a National flag so how could it have represented slavery or racism?"
"Please Doug, I only came in to get my teeth cleaned."
"Right, well put your head back and let's have a look. Open wide... So, how about Planned Parenthood hey? Bunch of baby murderers."

We found the boat on Craigslist and drove two hours to a small marina near D.C. to look it over. The 1997 Regal Commodore 242 cabin cruiser showed its age and there was a petrified fish in one of the cabin cupboards but the motor ran and it didn't sink during a test ride so we negotiated a fair price and towed the boat home. It was bigger and heavier than I'd anticipated and, as our vehicle has a towing capacity of two frozen chickens, the drive home took nearly seven hours. Going up hills was the worst; at one point we were passed by a jogger. He was one of those old, frail looking joggers with the wide crotch-height shorts that look like they're in it for distance rather than time. We passed him going down on the other side though, we were doing around 150mph as our brakes couldn't cope with the weight.

"What are we going to name it?"

"The boat? Whatever you want, Holly."

"I'm going to look up clever boat names online when we have reception. How long before we get out of these mountains?"

"Two or three more miles, so about an hour."

"The name needs to be witty. Like Vitamin C but instead of the letter C, we use the word Sea."

"Why would we call it Vitamin Sea?"

"I'm not saying we call it Vitamin Sea, I'm saying it has to be a play on words like that. Vitamin Sea would only make sense if we worked in the dietary supplement industry or if the boat was orange. How much would it cost to paint it?"

"We're not painting the boat orange, Holly."

"Fine. We have enough work to do on it before we can take it to the lake anyway. All the cabin upholstery needs to be replaced and it needs to be cleaned from top to bottom. It's disgusting."

"It *is* a bit of a bushpig... actually, that would..."

"We're not calling it Bushpig."

"Why not?"

"It's a derogatory Australian term for an ugly woman."

"No it isn't, it's a derogatory Australian term for a fat, dirty, ugly woman. It's funny."

"It's sexist and cruel. And stupid. Come on everyone, let's go for a ride on Bushpig. All aboard Bushpig!"

"So Bushpig it is then."

"We're not calling it Bushpig."

When we finally made it home, around 2am, we realized we hadn't taken the height of the trailer into account and Bushpig was three-feet taller than our garage door.

"We could try letting some of the air out of the tires."
"What good will that do, Holly?"
"I saw a show on HGTV where a couple bought a tiny home that they could tow around and they came to a low bridge and couldn't fit under it so they let some air out of the tires and were able to fit under easily."
"Prior to the air being let out, how much higher were they than the bridge clearance?"
"About an inch."
"Right, so we'll have flat tires but only two-feet, eleven-inches to worry about."
"Two-feet, *ten* inches. If they'd only lowered the tiny house one inch, it would have still scraped."

The driveway leading to our garage is only a car length and the trailer, well over thirty feet, would have stuck out into the middle of the street. As the driveway is on a forty-five degree incline, I've no idea how I would have gotten Bushpig up it anyway. I fell and slid once when the driveway was icy and picked up enough speed and momentum to make it all the way across the street. Parking Bushpig on the street wasn't an option either, as we live in an older area of town with no on-street parking. Around 3am, we towed Bushpig to JM and Lori's house, quietly uncoupled the trailer, and left it in their driveway.

"Hey, it's JM."

"Morning sunshine."

"Morning. I just made my myself a coffee and walked outside and there's a big ass boat in my driveway."

"Is there?"

"Yes. You wouldn't happen to know anything about that would you?"

"Maybe you won it in a raffle."

"I did actually buy a raffle ticket recently."

"Was it for a boat?"

"No, a ham."

"Did you check the back of the ticket? The boat might be second prize."

"It didn't fit through your garage door, did it?"

"No, we were about three-feet out. I tried letting some air out of the tires but that didn't work."

"Why didn't you just take it straight to the lake?"

"I need to work it on it first. The interior fabrics have to be replaced and the faucets in the galley and head* don't work for some reason. It also needs a good scrub. I'll work out somewhere to move it to today."

"It's fine where it is. It's a big driveway and we've got plenty of room to get the cars out. "

"Thanks, JM. It should only be there a week or two."

---

* *That's nautical-speak for bathroom. A tiny toilet and sink in an area half the size and height of most shower cubicles. Taking a dump in there is like doing Pilates inside a cardboard box that a washing machine came in.*

Bushpig stayed in JM and Lori's driveway for three months. We had the interior reupholstered with white marine vinyl within the first week. Even if the original blue with green and yellow confetti patterned fabric hadn't been ripped and faded, we would still have replaced it. It's been more than twenty years since I last caught public transport, because I'm not poor, but I have a vivid memory of the bus seats being the exact same pattern. I was going for a more contemporary look and I thought Holly was onboard with the design decision but then she bought four nautically themed throw-pillows at TJ Maxx. Two had fish on them, one had an anchor, and the fourth featured some kind of weird looking frog.

"What's with the weird looking frog?"
"It's nautical."
"Is it though? It looks like it's dancing. Or being flung from a trebuchet."
"We're keeping it."
"Can we at least turn it around so it's facing the seat or is there an even weirder frog on the other side?"
"I knew you wouldn't like it."
"What did you get it for then?"
"They only had two fish pillows and one anchor. It was either the frog or a New York taxi."
"What's in the other bag?"
" Just some soaps, candles, a bottle of olive oil with a sprig of rosemary in it, and a ceramic owl."

Cleaning Bushpig took an additional week. We went through six bottles of bleach inside the cabin, as I don't think the previous owners had ever cleaned. Walls we assumed were beige turned out to be white and cabinets we thought were white turned out to be a veneer of dry powdery mold. The mold inside the bar fridge was thick enough to easily remove in sheets like insulation batts but it took almost a full day to scrape away twenty-odd years of accumulated fecal splashes from the toilet before we could enter the head without dry-retching.

The compact microwave oven in the galley wasn't worth cleaning - the mesh in the door was rusty and when I tested it, my chest got warm. It came out easily and I replaced it with a new one - I know a guy named Gavin who works at Kmart and he sold me a Kenmore model in the parking lot for twenty-five-dollars.

I paid my friend Spencer to wash and polish the outside. He's poor so he did the whole hull for thirty-five dollars. I probably could have gotten away with paying him less but it took him twelve hours and I feel that's a fair price for his time. Often when I go camping with JM, Spencer tags along and I pay him to put up and take down my tent in Skittles. That might seem lazy but I'd honestly rather sleep in my car than put it up and take it down myself as it's over-engineered and has 798 tent poles of varying length and diameter.

The other advantage to Spencer joining us camping is that he and I have similar tastes in music. When it's just JM and I at camp, I have to listen to whiny songs about pickup trucks, working the land, and good-hearted women.

"Right, if you are going to bitch about the song so much, I'll change it."
"No, leave it, JM. If you change it now I'll never find out if the rain eventually came and saved his crops."
"It's not about the crops, it's about his love of the land."
"I thought it was about how much he enjoys driving his pickup with the window down."
"Yes, because he loves the land. Here, listen to this one..."
"It's the same song."
"No, it isn't. Just listen."
"I'm pretty sure you just hit repeat. I recognize that bottlecaps on a stick instrument."
"It's a different song, listen to the words goddammit. That's the problem with your beep beep boop computer music, you have no appreciation for well written lyrics with meaning."
"Is this one also about farming?"
"Shut the fuck up and listen to it. How can you criticize a song if you don't listen to the lyrics?"
"That's where our music requirements differ, I like a bit of bass with a drop and a tune. I don't give a fuck how much a farmer loves his land. I'd assume he'd get another job if he didn't."

"This song isn't about his love of the land. It's about his unrequited love for a diner waitress named Stacey."
"He's singing about tumbleweeds, they're fairly landish."
"Stacey's hair is the color of tumbleweeds. He didn't say he loves tumbleweeds. It's a metaphor."
"It's farm emo."
"Fuck you, I'm going to bed."

JM's favorite farm-emo singer is a hairy guy named David Allan Coe who looks like he probably owns a lot of guns and lives in a log cabin in the woods that his granpappy built. His most famous song, which I've heard far too many times, is about driving his pickup truck to collect his mother from prison on her release day but, before he gets there, she's run over by a train. It's pretty much up there with the classics like *Achy Breaky Heart* by Hannah Montana's dad and Kenny Chesney's *She Thinks My Tractor's Sexy*. For those not familiar with *She Thinks My Tractor's Sexy*, here are the lyrics:

Plowing these fields in the hot summer sun.
Over by the gate yonder here she comes.
With a basket full of chicken,
and a big cold jug of sweet tea.
I make a little room and she climbs on up,
I open up the throttle and stir a little dust.
Look at her face, she ain't a foolin' me,
she thinks my tractor's sexy.
It really turns her on.

It's basically the musical equivalent of *Fifty Shades of Grey* for farmers. Yes, Cletus, everyone thinks your tractor is hot. And your oversized Carhartt jacket and Wrangler boot-cut jeans with pig shit stains on the cuffs. When you're blocking traffic doing 15mph on a single lane road, we're definitely all thinking, "I'd love to give that tractor driver some chicken," and not, "Pull over and let us pass, you leather-faced old fuck, we've got places to be."

I realize without farmers we wouldn't have corn on the cob or watermelons, but that's no reason to pretend there's anything appealing about their lifestyle, appearance, machinery, or music.

The only farming-related song I do like is the one that goes, "You don't have to be lonely, at Farmersonly.com." It's pretty catchy and the video clip has fat girls wearing rubber boots and milking cows - which covers two of my three fetishes.

We can't all have the same tastes in music though. I grew up in the 80s listening to New Order and Visage while JM grew up listening to his grandmother screaming, "Your pigs are loose again, JM!"

I also grew up around boats. I realize that makes it sound like I lived on a pier or something but that's fine, I'd quite like to live on a pier. Away from the area where they cut up fish obviously but close enough to watch the boats coming in and going out. My grandfather regularly took me fishing on his wooden skiff when I was very young. It was an old boat and you couldn't wear shorts on it or you'd get splinters, but it floated. My main job was to bait hooks and untangle fishing lines because my grandfather had failing eyesight and arthritis in both hands. Sometimes he'd let me drive while he fished and he taught me how to dock. As we approached a pier, I'd jump off the boat and my grandfather would throw me a rope to loop around a pillar. Sometimes I'd miss the rope and he'd yell, "You wee useless cunt!" He wasn't Scottish, just a dick.

He also showed me how to tie several knots but I've forgotten them all now. I usually just use ratchet straps anyway. If I do have to tie a knot, I just tie several granny knots over the top of each other and figure they'll squeeze together to form the world's best knot.

"Is this rope tangled?"
"No, Holly, that's a sailor's knot. A Sheep's Hitch Double Shot knot."
"Did you just make that up?"
"No."
"It sounds made up."
"Well it's not. My grandfather taught me it."
"How do I get it undone."
"Ah, there's a bit of a trick to it. You'll need a pair of needle nosed pliers or a sharp knife."

My father also owned a boat - a speedboat that we towed to 'the spot' on the River Murray on summer weekends. He named it *Phil's Thrills & Spills,* which is a bit lame because his name was Phil. He let me drive it once and I did fairly well so he let me dock it. There's quite a bit of difference between a ten horsepower wooden skiff and a four hundred horsepower power boat. I wasn't allowed to drive it again. We had water skis and tubes but the best water-toy we owned was an inflatable Coleman queen-sized camping mattress. If the boat went fast enough, the person being towed on the mattress could lift the front to catch air and sometimes get as high as thirty feet.

Almost every major injury I had in my youth was boating related so I understand how dangerous they can be. From slipping on wet decks to getting limbs caught between boat and dock, I broke fourteen bones over the years. Nine were in a single accident when the rope towing the inflatable Coleman queen-sized camping mattress snapped and I hit the front window of a passing houseboat.

Another time, when I was sitting at the bow while at high speed, my father hit a sandbar and I was thrown into a willow tree. Nobody wants to be in water under a willow tree - it's where the monsters live - so I credit terror for my managing to swim back to the boat with a broken arm and a tree branch through my shoulder.

I've seen worse boating injuries though; once when my cousin Susan came to the river with us, she lost her balance as my father powered up, fell off the back, and hit her leg on the propeller. It looked like a shark had bitten a three-inch chunk out of her calf and just left splintered bone. It was the first time Susan had been to the river and she never went back. I think she had some kind of social anxiety disorder. My sister told me that they repaired the hole in Susan's leg with meat taken from her bottom, which I believed for thirty years until she told me she'd made it up. She also told me that when I turned ten, I'd be able to teleport short distances but it was a closely guarded secret from under-tens for their own good because they needed to learn how to walk and run first.

"Holly, you know what would have been a better name for the boat than Bushpig?"
"Anything at all?"
"No, That'll Do, Pig."
"The thing the farmer says at the end of *Babe*?"
"Yes."
"That's actually perfect. I love it. We should definitely name the boat that."
"Too late, I've already registered it and organized a boat slip at Smith Mountain Lake under the name Bushpig."
"Well change it."
"You can't change a boat's name. It's bad luck."
"Who says?"
"Sailors. The boat sinks or someone drowns."

"Since when are you superstitious?"

"I'm not about ladders and cats but boat safety isn't worth fucking with. Do you want the boat to sink or someone to drown?"

"No."

"Did I tell you what happened to my cousin Susan?"

"Yes, her entire leg and half her pelvis got chopped off by a propeller blade. I'm sure you exaggerated though."

"Well, I didn't. She has a robot leg now."

Apparently it is possible to change a boat's name but it requires a lengthy chat with Poseidon and splashing stuff about which seems like more effort than it's worth. Besides, after arguing for the name Bushpig, I wasn't about to admit that I hated it too.

Bushpig was ready for the water after three weeks but we were waiting on a pump to be delivered and installed before we towed it to the lake - after changing fuses and checking wiring, the cause of the faucets not functioning was traced to a faulty fresh water pump located under a cover in the floor of the dining area. The compartment in which it was mounted, about the size of a laundry sink, was full of water as the pump had rusted out and leaked badly. I siphoned the water and removed the pump from its mounting bracket with a cordless screwdriver. The bracket was also rusty so I unscrewed it as well and noticed water had managed to make its way behind it. Hence my trip to Lowe's to buy a spray can of Flex Seal.

The replacement pump, a Shurflo Aqua King II, arrived three days later. I could have had it in two but I hate paying for shipping on Amazon Prime.

Holly and I both have Amazon Prime accounts - I realize it would be cheaper to share one account but there's no way Holly is having access to my purchase history. Even the 'recently viewed items' section would probably mean several uncomfortable chats. It's not that I'm into anything particularly unusual, it's just that when I search for an item on Amazon, say a book on boat maintenance, it comes up with a 'customers who bought this item also bought' panel and I'm suddenly invested in Jack64's opinion of a 22-foot multi-use ladder with 300-pound rating or Lisa G's review with photos of a toenail clipper. I don't write the algorithms so don't blame me if it shows yodeling pickles or men's leotards.

Holly dragged me to a networking event recently and Doug the grand-wizard dentist was there. I forget what the networking event was for but, as we live in a small town, the same dreadful people are at every event so it hardly matters. I know an old guy named Dick who regularly hosts an event called The Cigar Club and it's honestly the saddest thing I have every seen. It's held in a venue where you're not allowed to smoke and it's usually just Dick and two or three old women sitting in a booth staring at each other.

"Ah, David, glad you could join us! Scoot over Gwen and let David in. We were just discussing Ruth's swollen fingers."
"Actually, I'm just here to meet someone at the bar."
"Fantastic, we'll come over and join you."
"Please don't, Dick."

Holly and I made the mistake of attending one of Dick's *Sounds Like Christmas!* parties one year. It was in a large hall but there were only ten people including Holly and myself. Dick and the other seven geriatrics stood on a podium and sang songs about Jesus at us until I convinced Holly that I was going to start breaking stuff if we didn't leave.

I just asked Holly what the networking event was for and she replied "Carpets and floor tiles I think." Which may give some idea of how exciting these things are but it doesn't explain why Doug was there or why he felt the need to share his opinion on transgender welfare recipients molesting children in public bathrooms. When he wandered off to get a drink and left his iPhone at our table, I discovered it was unlocked and one-click Amazon Prime ordering was turned on so I ordered thirty-six yodeling pickles, eighteen pairs of boys briefs, five cat blankets, and a copy of Charlotte Snape's novel *Bat Boy* - a gay baseball romance. Hopefully it messed up his algorithms for months.

Lori was home alone the day I drove over to their house to install the new water pump on the boat. She doesn't work and they have a cleaner so I think she just talks to her cat and watches Hallmark Channel all day. She used to be on the board of a community group that organized Christmas decorations for lamp posts but the two-hour meeting once a year took too much time out of her heavy schedule. She does occasionally leave the house but only after two or three days of extensive planning - the time Lori and JM joined us on the houseboat took two months of scheduling, eight meetings, and a seventy-four page document covering everything from required outfits to sunscreen SPF ratings. It was spiral bound and featured checklists, maps, emergency numbers, GPS locations and clip-art of ducks.

"It's a few nights on a houseboat, Lori, what's with the eight large suitcases?"
"It's all I could fit in the car. I had to leave two suitcases behind so it better not snow."
"It's ninety-degrees. What's in the plastic grocery bag?"
"JM's stuff."

I said hello to Lori and left her to her Hallmark movie. It was something about a wedding planner from a big city who drives to another city but breaks down on the way and has to stay a week in a small-town bed and breakfast run by a handsome widower and his six-year-old daughter who saw a falling star and wished she had a mom.

I only watched a few minutes of it but I caught the gist. Basically if you replace the wedding planner with a busy advertising executive or materialistic socialite, and the bed and breakfast with a Christmas-tree farm or country vet, you have every Hallmark movie ever made.

With my tool bag, the pump, and a can of Flex Seal, I climbed up onto Bushpig and made my way into the cabin. It was an unusually warm day for late March and I was wearing a t-shirt and cargo shorts.

I get a bit of flack for wearing cargo shorts but I'll choose six handy pockets over being fashionable any day of the week. I wore cargo shorts to a wedding once. I ironed them though. I honestly believe the world would be a much happier place if everyone suddenly decided, "Six handy pockets. I get it now. I'm never wearing anything else again." The saddest day of each year for me is when I leave the house in cargo shorts and realize my legs are cold. It's all downhill from there and I have to search for trousers in the back of the wardrobe. I realize cargo shorts also come in pant length but I wouldn't be seen dead in public wearing cargo pants. I know a guy named Nick who wears cargo pants and he shoots pumpkins behind his trailer with an AR-15 semi-automatic rifle.

I lifted the cover of the pump compartment and gave the can of Flex Seal a good shake before spraying liberally. I used almost half the can on the area where the mount was to be reinstalled and, figuring it wouldn't hurt to give the entire space a waterproof coating, used the rest of the can on the floor and walls of the compartment. The mount went back on easily, over the top of the still wet Flex Seal to create a good seal, and the replacement pump connected to that without any trouble. I was in the process of screwing in the last bolt when the cordless screwdriver created a spark.

Apparently the highly flammable propellant used in highly flammable Flex Seal is heavier than the air around it, and the gas collected in the sunken compartment. I was on my knees with my head about a foot from the space and my arms inside when the gas ignited and a fireball engulfed me. I remember, as the intense heat ripped into me, thinking, "So this is how I die, in an explosion."

It wasn't the first time I've been on fire. I lost some hair and my eyebrows last autumn after Seb poured several gallons of gasoline into a 40-gallon drum filled with leaves while I was inside looking for a lighter, and, when I was about ten, I tried to breathe fire by spraying a mouthful of gasoline at a candle and burnt my mouth and most of a shed. I must have yelled in surprise and sucked back some of the fuel and flames because I couldn't speak or eat solid food for weeks and lost my sense of smell for several years.

Also, when I was twelve, a friend of mine named Wilson invented Tennis Ball.

"You know what would be an awesome game, David?"
"What?"
"Tennis, but you play it at night by dipping the tennis ball in petrol and lighting it."
"Sounds a bit dangerous."
"No, it wouldn't be. We'd wear a fireproof glove to pick the ball up with. My dad has a leather glove near our fireplace that you can pick up burning logs with."
"Well as long as we have a fireproof glove I can't see how anything could go wrong. We should call it Fireball Tennis."
"No, we're not calling it that. I invented the game so I get to name it."
"Fine. What are we are going to call it then?"
"Something like... Fire Tennis."
"That's just my name without the ball bit."
"No it isn't, okay, what's something like a fireball but isn't the word fireball... like... a ball of fire."
"Comets are balls of fire. We could call it Comet Ball."
"I was just about to come up with that and now we can't use it. Besides, it's still tennis, we have to have the word tennis in the name... like instead of Comet Ball, it could be... Tennis Ball."
"Tennis Ball?"
"Yes, because it needs to say tennis and we play it with a ball."
"It doesn't say anything about the ball being on fire."
"It doesn't need to, we know the ball is on fire. It's my game and we're calling it Tennis Ball."

Despite the fireproof gloves, Tennis Ball was actually pretty dangerous. I think we may have soaked the ball for too long but I'm not sure that made a difference. Wilson slept over and we snuck out my window that night with two tennis rackets, a tennis ball, and an ice-cream container of petrol we'd drained from a leaf-blower. There were tennis courts at the end of our street; my father had been a member there for several years until he ran off with the lady that did the club fees. Lighting the tennis ball went off without a hitch and Wilson ran with it to the other side of the court to serve. Forgoing the bounce, he threw the ball high and slammed it with his tennis racket. I definitely had the best view from my side of the court. The fireball was probably twenty feet in diameter; splashes of fire made the net. Wilson started blistering on the walk home so when we got back, he laid on the grass and I turned the sprinkler on for him.

The fire in Bushpig was actually more of a flash than an explosion, and more of a 'whoomph' than a 'kaboom', but it was violent enough to throw me backwards. The smell and sound of burning hair alerted me to the fact that I was on fire and I ran my hands over my head frantically to extinguish the flames. Fire raged in the sunken compartment and thick black smoke filled the cabin as I made my way out onto the deck. There were two mandatory fire-extinguishers onboard, one was inside the cabin, cut off by flames, the other was deckside inside a life-vest cubby and readily accessible.

I managed to free the extinguisher from its cradle and pull the pin out. I was shaking, probably due to adrenalin, but I wasn't in a lot of pain. At that point, it just felt like a 'buzzing static' type of bad sunburn. I aimed the nozzle inside the cabin and emptied the entire contents, making sure the fire was completely out before climbing off the boat. I was half way down the ladder when the pain hit. It was as if a thousand wasps were attacking my hands, arms and face. Wasps on fire, with lava for venom. My vision blurred and my legs buckled but I made it to the back door of Lori and JM's house and knocked.

JM and Lori have told me a dozen times that I don't need to knock before I enter but I can't walk into anybody's house without doing so. Years ago, after visiting my friend Geoffrey, I realized I'd left my sunglasses at his house and went back. I'd only been gone a few minutes so I walked straight in to discover Geoffrey taking a dump in his kitchen trashcan. It was one of those flip up lid kind and Geoffrey was squatting over it, naked from the waist down, pressing the foot pedal down with his hand. As he yelled and leapt up in surprise, the lid closed and a half-out log broke off and landed on top. Nothing prepares you for this kind of social interaction so I just stood there staring at the poo on the lid while Geoffrey screamed at me for not knocking. Apparently the plumbing in his toilet wasn't working or something but who shits in a trashcan? Shit in the shower and waffle-stomp those nuggets down the drain like the rest of us.

I realize the likelihood of walking in on JM or Lori while they're taking a trash can dump is slim but it can't be completely ruled out. I lock the doors when I'm home because Holly's father, Tom, once poked his head into the bathroom while I was in the shower and said, "Just dropping off a watermelon."

"Lori, can I come in? I was on fire."
"It's open... oh my god."
"Yes, it hurts a lot. Can I use your sink to splash water on myself?"
"Well sure but you're bright red and blistering. Should I call an ambulance?"
"No, I just need to cool my face and arms down. How do I turn this faucet on?"
"It's a touch faucet, you just touch it."
"Like this?"
"No, on the top."
"Here?"
"No, down a bit... closer to the middle. No? Try a light tap instead of slapping it."

JM and Lori have a lot of complicated gadgets in their home. I watered their plants once while they were away and it took me an hour to work out the door locks. It requires two keys to be turned simultaneously, like a missile bunker, while entering a sixteen-digit code with a stick held in your teeth. If you get it wrong, poisonous gas sprays out of a nozzle.

Lori rang Holly and JM while I splashed water on my face and arms. It helped with the pain somewhat but the skin on my arms started to peel away under the stream of running water. JM arrived well before Holly. I've long suspected he has some kind of underground tunnel between his house and business premises so he can slip home for snacks and naps.

"Oh my god."
"Yes, it hurts a lot, JM."
"You need to go to the hospital."
"That's not happening. The health care system in this country is a joke. What does my hair look like?"
"I wouldn't be worried about your hair, you have second or third degree burns. I'm calling an ambulance."
"I think it's actually starting to feel a bit better. How burnt is my hair? Is it missing chunks?"
"There isn't any hair. Just blisters."
"Are you serious?"
"It's probably all that hairspray you use."
"I don't use hairspray. I use American Crew Low Shine Fiber. It's like a putty. Do you have a hand mirror?"
"I've got my phone camera, hang on... here, you go."
"Oh my god."

Holly rode in the ambulance with me. My fingers looked like sausages on arrival at the hospital and they had to cut off my wedding ring. I don't remember much after that because they had to intubate me for the helicopter ride.

"Like a baby chicken?"

"Sorry?"

"Why do I have to be incubated?"

"Intubate, not incubate. We're going to put a breathing tube down your throat."

"That doesn't sound good. Is it necessary?"

"Yes. We're flying you to the burn unit in Richmond and you need to be sedated for the trip. You might feel a small sting... Okay, on a scale of one to ten, how would you describe your current pain?"

"I've had some pretty bad toothaches before so probably a nine."

"And now?"

"About a five... maybe a two. Actually, I feel really good."

"You might want to lie back."

"I'd rather sit up, I haevs shimmobive wht hapnig..."

It wasn't the first time I've been in a helicopter. Years ago, when I was working at de Masi jones, a client requested aerial photographs of a vineyard for their website redesign. That kind of thing is now commonly done with drones but we didn't have them in the 'olden days' of 2006. We were in the air for just over an hour and were charged *three-hundred-dollars*. My helicopter flight from the Harrisonburg hospital to the Richmond burn unit, a twenty minute trip, cost $54,217.00 - I checked on EBay and I can buy a used helicopter for $43,000.00 which would leave me $11,217.00 for lessons and one of those helmets with the sunshades built in.

PHI AIR MEDICAL

BEYOND THE CALL

04/02/18

David R Thorne

Patient: David Thorne
Date of Service: 03/29/18
Account#: ██████
Account Balance: $54,217.00

Dear David Thorne,

I have been selected as your personal Patient Advocate for PHI Air Medica, the company that was called to transport you to the hospital.

My role is to answer any questions you may have about the transport and billing processes. Also to:
- Assist you in understanding your rights and responsibilities
- Handle any unresolved issues
- Determine your benefits through any insurance you may have
- Handle the settlement of your bill

Our promise and commitment to you is to help you settle your account balance in a way that works best for your financial situation and so that your account will continue to remain in good standing.
As your personal Patient Advocate, I am here to assist you in resolving your account balance.

In the upcoming weeks you may receive correspondence from your insurance carrier or PHI Air Medical. It is important you review the documents and contact our office related to the documents received. We can assist in determining if additional steps are required to resolve the billing process.

If you have a PHI Cares™ membership we encourage you to call us at the number listed below and provide the membership number so we can better assist you with your account.

Your willingness to answer our calls, questions and letters in a timely manner means that you will remain in good standing with our company as we work to settle the balance of your bill.

I encourage you or a family member to call me at 800-421-6111 at the extension below to ask any questions or relay any concerns you may have.

In Service,

Crystal S. Ext 3005
Patient Advocate

From: David Thorne
Date: Friday 6 April 2018 2.12pm
To: info@phihelico.com
Subject: Helicopter

Dear Phi,

I'd like to cancel my order please. I have no room for a helicopter and did not authorize this purchase.

Regards, David Thorne

Phi didn't reply to my email but I thought I'd add it to show I tried. I received an automated response telling me to call a Patient Advocate but when I called the number, all their Patient Advocates were busy and I was placed in a queue. The estimated wait time was forty-seven minutes, which is about forty-six minutes and forty-five seconds longer than I'm prepared to listen to Michael Bublé on hold. I was all riled up when I rang but after fifteen seconds of *Haven't Met You Yet*, I was honestly happy to pay fifty-four thousand just for the experience to end. It's a tactic that could be used in any negotiation.

"We will never sign such a disproportionate agreement."
"Okay, that's completely up to you. I'm going to need you to listen to this CD of Michael Bublé's Sinatra covers before you leave though. It's a new protocol we have."
"Fine."
Fly me to the moon...
"I'll sign."

Coming from a country where the health care system *isn't* based on buying insurance company CEO's their third vacation home in the Hamptons, I simply couldn't wrap my head around the amount until I showed the invoice to JM and he explained, "That's because America's helicopter pilots are the best in the world."

He then jumped a monster truck, with Kid Rock in the back singing *Born Free,* over twelve exploding school buses full of Mexican children. There were fireworks and eagles and afterwards, everyone ate at Chick-fil-A.

I was kept unconscious for three days. At some point during that time, someone stuck a tube up my penis. It must have gone in about three feet because the removal was fairly traumatic. Holly was standing beside my bed when I awoke. She was there every day so I've decided to keep her. Of course if we'd never met, I wouldn't have bought a boat so there is that. She asked me once what I'd be doing if we hadn't met and apparently, "Sitting sad and alone in a dark room knowing a part of me is missing." is the correct answer, not, "Same shit, less noise."

Each day, my bandages were removed, my skin scrubbed with a scourer, then I was bandaged back up. It wasn't as pleasant as it sounds. Holly helped me eat and drink and urinate into a plastic bottle but I wasn't about to have her wipe my arse so I just held it for fifteen days. We've been together ten years and I still pretend I don't fart.

Holding your bowels for fifteen days apparently does strange things to both the body and mind, I had hiccups for six days straight and experienced vivid hallucinations. At one point I was convinced that I was in some kind of simulation which was glitching. Windows changed location, walls flickered, and nurses said things like, "Okay, I'm just going to check check check check check your blood pressure." as if caught in a loop. I told one of the nurses that I was fully aware she was a simulation so she may as well stop pretending and everything froze, rewound a few seconds, then played back out. I blinked and was home in bed. Holly was beside me watching television and I sat up staring at her confused.

"What's wrong?"
"How did I get here? I was in the hospital. Or maybe a simulation of a hospital."
"You were dreaming. Go back to sleep."
"I wasn't in a fire? It was so vivid. I was working on the boat and there was an accident and I burnt my face and arms. Did we buy a boat?"
"No. Why would we buy a boat?"
"You've no idea how relieved I am. It was honestly the most realistic dream I've ever had. Every day they scoured off the blisters and scabs and I couldn't wipe my own arse."
"Okay, I'm just going to check check check check check your blood pressure."
"Oh no."

It could have been worse of course, there were people in the intensive care unit that looked like they were made out of wax and the patient in the room next to me, an eighty-year-old man named Dennis, was burnt so badly in a turkey-fryer accident that both his arms had to be amputated. They drew the curtains when they cleaned his torso but there was a gap at the bottom and I could see chunks of flesh attached to bandages as they dropped to the floor. It smelled like burnt pork. When I was eventually able to leave my bed and walk around the ward - holding my bandaged arms above my head to prevent blood rushing to my hands - Dennis asked me if I was his wife so he was either on decent painkillers or his wife wasn't much of a looker. I hadn't seen anyone visit him so I watched television in his room for a bit while he drifted in and out of consciousness. He told me that he enjoyed gardening and had just bought a new shovel. He also told me that the color of his curtains kept changing.

"We'd know if it was."
"Not necessarily, Dennis. The simulation would create boundaries to prevent us finding out. Imagine you're driving down a highway and you pass a field with trees in the middle of it. You tell yourself that you could stop the car and get out and walk towards the trees but you don't. There's no reason to stop, you have places to be, and it's someone else's property. What if you did stop though and walked towards the trees and the closer you got, the more pixelated they became?"

"I bought a new shovel last week."
"Yes, you told me that. Did you keep the receipt?"

I vaguely remember some commotion that night but a nurse closed my curtains. Dennis wasn't in his room the next day and when I asked if he'd been moved, I was told that he'd died. It may be a dreadful thing to say but his injuries made me feel a lot better about my own. Or at least realize just how lucky I had been. I hadn't lost any limbs and, as the burns on my face were mostly superficial, I didn't look like one of those marine veterans who has been on fire and lost their nose and ears but their fiancé still marries. I took a stroll through the children's burn ward afterwards to make myself feel even better. Some of those kids were really fucked up.

I left against medical advice. Both my hands were still bandaged and I felt a little rough, but I honestly couldn't stay another day in that hospital. For all the arguments about America having the best health care in the world, Richmond's VCU is like an Australian hospital from 1975. The beds need to be taken out the back and burnt. It's a two-hour drive from Richmond to Harrisonburg, through rural areas with farms and pastures backing onto the Blue Ridge Mountains. As we passed a field with trees in the middle of it, I asked Holly to pull over and got out. I intended to walk all the way to the trees but about thirty feet from the car, the field got marshy and I was only wearing hospital slippers so I went back.

"What was the point of that?"

"Nothing. Just thought I'd get some fresh air after being stuck in the hospital for six months."

"It was only two weeks."

"It felt like six months. It was dreadful."

"I know it was. The brain has a way of filing certain experiences in a 'just don't think about it' box though. In a few months you'll hardly remember it."

"I doubt that very much."

"You'd be surprised. It's like when you got me the vacuum cleaner for my birthday."

"How is receiving a vacuum cleaner comparable to being burnt?"

"It's not. I'm just saying bad experiences eventually get filed in a 'just don't think about it' box."

"And your box has a vacuum cleaner in it?"

"Among other things."

"Are they all electrical appliances?"

"No."

"Give me an example."

"Just stuff. Like when we argue."

"Ah. I see where the problem is. I don't call mine a 'just don't think about it' box, I call it my 'that was pointless, what did I miss on television' box."

"Nice. You do realize I drove two hours each way to be with you in the hospital every day don't you? It wasn't easy for me either."

"Put it in your 'just don't think about it' box. With the vacuum cleaner."

In my defense, how many vacuum cleaners are guaranteed to never lose suction and have a big ball instead of wheels? And, if someone asks what you want for your birthday and you state, "You don't need to get me anything this year, just a nice dinner somewhere," there's no way for that person to know that this means, "Just a Tiffany tennis bracelet, thanks." Also, there's nothing wrong with Qdoba. They make a decent burrito. It's not a fast-food restaurant because they don't have a drive-thru.

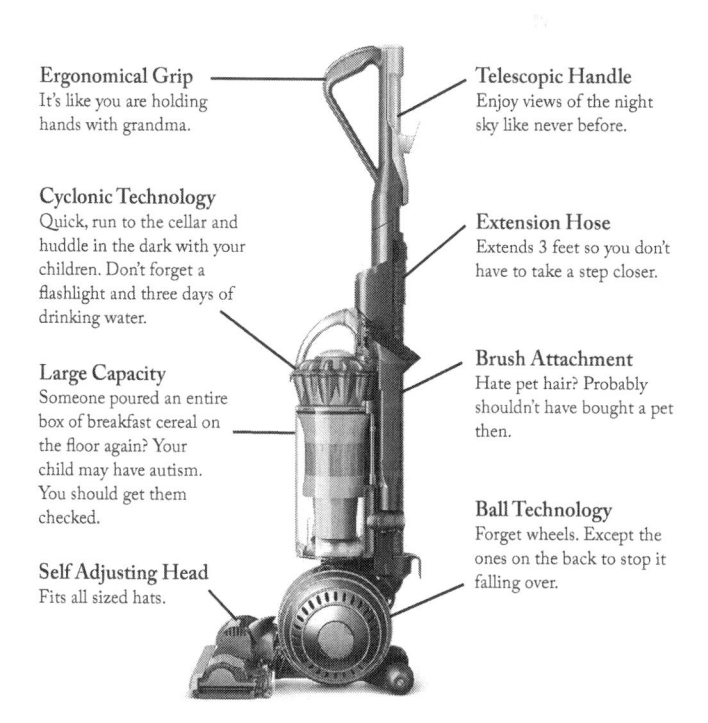

Ergonomical Grip
It's like you are holding hands with grandma.

Cyclonic Technology
Quick, run to the cellar and huddle in the dark with your children. Don't forget a flashlight and three days of drinking water.

Large Capacity
Someone poured an entire box of breakfast cereal on the floor again? Your child may have autism. You should get them checked.

Self Adjusting Head
Fits all sized hats.

Telescopic Handle
Enjoy views of the night sky like never before.

Extension Hose
Extends 3 feet so you don't have to take a step closer.

Brush Attachment
Hate pet hair? Probably shouldn't have bought a pet then.

Ball Technology
Forget wheels. Except the ones on the back to stop it falling over.

The brain does actually have a way of filing certain experiences in a 'just don't think about it' box. I no longer jolt awake during the night and run my hands through my hair to put out the fire. I had to wear a baseball cap for a few months but hair grows back. It was actually looking good for a while but then I cut it. I have some scarring on my arms and my left hand doesn't work very well, but I never really used it that much anyway and it's a good excuse for not pitching my own tent when I go camping.

"I'd do it myself, Spencer, but I was burnt terribly in a boat fire and no longer have full use of my left hand."
"Yes, I know you were burnt. You don't have to say the whole sentence about boat fires and hands every time."
"Hand, not hands. It's just the left hand that I no longer have full use of. I guess I could probably manage."
"No, I'll do it for you."
"Thanks, Spencer. How many bags of Skittles do I owe you now?"
"Eight. And a full size Snickers for blowing up your air mattress."
"I'll remember the pump next time."
"You said that last time."
"Yes, well, I've had a few things on mind, Spencer. I was burnt terribly in a boat fire and no longer have full use of my left hand. But yes, I probably should have stopped, dropped and rolled and then grabbed the air pump and put it in my car so I wouldn't forget it. How many Skittles will it take for you to carry me to my tent?"

Spencer is approximately eighteen-feet tall and has lungs the size of a hippopotamus so filling a mattress is really only worth a bite-sized Snickers. A full-size Snickers is bite-sized to Spencer though. A puppy could fit inside his mouth. He used to work as a pool lifeguard at Massanutten resort but every time he jumped in, they had to refill the pool. I've lived in Massanutten and I know what they charge for water. They had to let him go after he snapped and threw a black kid into the deep end.

A few months after the accident, when I was feeling up to the task, I drove to clean up the mess in Bushpig and discovered Joe and Andrew - Lori and JM's offspring - had already vacuumed the fire-extinguisher residue and cleaned the area of soot. They'd also finished hooking up the water pump, which was nice of them. I checked the clamps just in case because they're both huge fuckups.

As JM owns a pickup truck, he offered to tow the boat to the lake so we made a road trip out of it. It meant listening to farm emo but it also meant going faster than walking speed. Halfway to the lake, we heard a squealing sound and JM turned down the stereo to ask, "What the fuck is that?" just as a trailer wheel came off and hurtled past us. It made it about three hundred feet down the road before hitting a bank, jumping over a wire fence, and coming to rest in the middle of a field. A couple of cows walked over to have a look so it probably made their day. I can't imagine they get much stimulation.

The three-wheeled trailer - previously four-wheeled - was a tad lop-sided and the boat sat at a jaunty angle, but it was still towable. The wheel had come off at the hub (which was glowing red when we climbed out to have a look), so it couldn't be put back on, but I climbed the fence to retrieve it anyway. It took a while because one of the cows stood its ground. I had to go back to the truck to get a bottle of water to squirt at it. Also, as I was climbing back over the fence, my t-shirt got caught on barbed wire and I had to rip it free. I was fairly annoyed about it because I'd taken the sleeves in that morning on Holly's sewing machine. I'm not a fan of t-shirt sleeves that stick out like bat wings. Or Gildan. Sometimes I'll see a t-shirt I like then discover the tag says Gildan and be furious that it wasted my time and interest. They're made out of fiberglass and staples and shrink to 1/8th of their original size when washed.

With only three trailer wheels, we had to drop our speed and didn't make it to the lake until dark. The owner of the marina where I'd rented a boat slip had gone home but I called him and he told me to put the boat in the water, tie it to the dock, and he'd take care of it the next morning. I'd been hoping to take the boat out for a short cruise but at least it was at the marina and would be ready for Holly and I to take out the next weekend. Neither JM or I had backed a boat down a boat-ramp before but it only took fourteen tries. With the rear wheels of the truck submerged and a cheer, the boat floated free of the trailer.

The slip rental included a parking area to leave the trailer. JM pulled it out of the water and uncoupled it while I secured the boat to the dock with ropes. There were three cleats on the side of Bushpig and I used about thirty granny knots on each to make it sure it wouldn't float away. On the way home, about thirty minutes from the lake, JM and I stopped in a town called Bedford and had a beer and hot pretzel at a small brewery called Beale's. They sold t-shirts with their logo on them but I didn't buy one because the tag said Gildan.

I'd brought along a light jacket for the road trip and put it on before going into the brewery. It was summer and too warm for a jacket but the burns on my arms were still quite evident at that stage and I was slightly self-conscious about them. I hadn't worn the jacket since the day Holly and I bought the boat - the day the guy who sold it to us had handed me the title, keys, and drain plug.

The drain plug is a fairly important component of boating. It's a hefty but short bolt, about an inch in diameter and length, located at the back of the boat in the hull. It's important to remove the drain plug when trailering a boat as it allows water that has collected in the bilge during boating to drain and prevents water collecting in the bilge from rain while being stored. It's just as important, and the first item on every boating check-list, to remember to put the drain plug back in before launching a boat. Otherwise the boat sinks.

JM said it was it the best hot pretzel he's ever had which had to have been an exaggeration. It was okay but the mustard it came with was just squeezed out of a Heinz mustard bottle and I prefer honey mustard with my pretzels. We finished our beer and I paid the tab.

"Seriously, best pretzel I've ever had."
"Yes, not bad."
"You didn't like your pretzel?"
"I didn't say that. It was actually a pretty decent pretzel."
"Too salty for you?"
"No, I like a lot of salt on my pretzels."
"Then what's the problem?"
"There isn't one. It wasn't the best pretzel I've ever had but there wasn't anything wrong with it. It might make it onto my top ten pretzel list if I had one but it wouldn't be in the top position. Maybe I've just had more pretzels than you."
"Well that's bullshit. I love pretzels."
"Then I guess I'm just more of a pretzel connoisseur. With a more advanced pretzel palette."
"That's a joke. You smoke cigarettes. I'm surprised you have any taste buds left at all."
"You chew tobacco. I'm surprised you still have lips."
"Why are you always so argumentative?"
"Me? You're the one outraged that I didn't think the pretzel was the culinary equivalent of *She Thinks My Tractor's Sexy*."
"Shut the fuck up and get in the truck."
"Hang on, I'm going to have a quick cigarette first."

My cigarettes were in a pocket of my cargo shorts but my lighter wasn't. I patted my shorts, then my jacket, and felt something in the right-hand pocket.

"How could you forget to put in the drain plug?"
"It was dark and I was tired after the long drive. Can you drive a bit faster?"
"What you need, is some kind of checklist."
"Yes, that's a good idea. Very helpful."
"A checklist with 'put in the drain plug' as the first item."
"You'd never even heard of a drain plug until ten minutes ago so don't act like you're Captain Nemo."
"The fish?"
"Yes, the fish. How long before we get there?"
"Twenty minutes. How long will the boat take to sink?"
"I've no idea, I've never timed it."
"The *Titanic* took two hours and forty minutes to sink."
"Is that right?"
"Yes, I watched a documentary last week on the History channel. If they'd just stayed straight instead of turning to avoid the iceberg, they wouldn't have sunk at all."
"Good to know. I'll keep that in mind."
"It took us thirty minutes to get to Bedford and we were in Beale's for almost an hour, so, if it takes thirty minutes to get back, that will still give us forty minutes before the boat sinks."
"Based on how long the *Titanic* took to go under? It was a much bigger boat."
"Yes, but it was also a lot heavier."

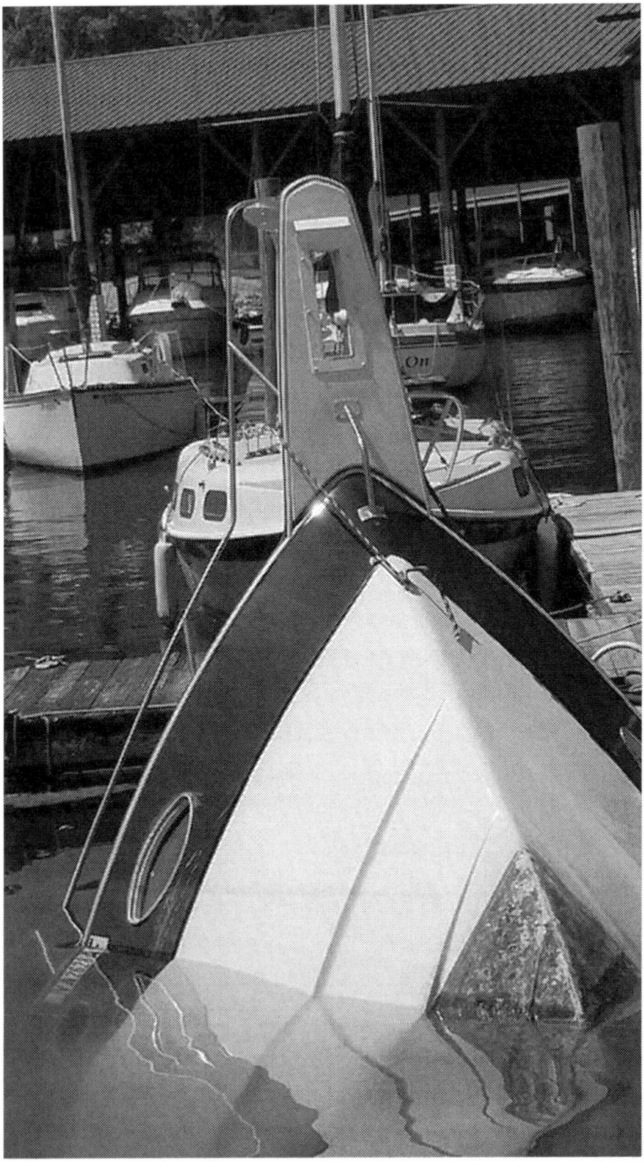

I've no idea how long it took Bushpig to sink but it was less than the *Titanic*. We stood on the dock watching bubbles break on the surface - most were steady runs as trapped air trickled through small gaps but occasionally there was a big 'bloop'. *Bushpig's* bow stuck out of the water four or five feet but the rest was completely submerged. We had to be careful where we stood as a large section of the dock had been ripped away - a credit to my knot-tying abilities. An Igloo cooler popped out of the water, startling us both. I tried to reach it with a plank from the broken dock but I knocked the lid open and it filled with water and sank.

"Hey. Just calling to check how you're going."
"All good."
"Did you get the boat into the water?"
"Yes."
"Are you on your way home?"
"Yes."
"You're being very short. Is everything's okay?"
"Everything's fine. Long day."
"Are you going to stop for dinner on your way home?"
"No, I had a pretzel."
"Was it good?"
"It was alright."
"Okay, I'll see you in a while. Tell JM to drive safely."
"I will. Oh, hey, is the boat insured?"
"Yes, why?"
"No reason. Bye."

I was planning to tell Holly when I got home but Lori called JM while we were still an hour from home and he told her what had happened. With Lori knowing, fifty other people knew within minutes and someone posted on Holly's Facebook page, "Sorry to hear about your boat. Thoughts and prayers."

I once bumped into Lori at a supermarket, while I was grabbing a few things on my way home, and before I got to the next aisle, Holly messaged me, "What do you have four loaves of bread in your cart for? We don't need that much bread."

I spoke to the owner of the marina the next morning. He seemed rather blasé about the whole thing so I asked him if it happened often and he said it didn't. I also asked him if he thought the boat would be okay and he laughed.

Our insurance agency covered the cost of having the boat raised and removed. And the dock repairs. The cost to repair a waterlogged twenty-year-old cabin cruiser is apparently greater than its worth so they wrote the boat off and wrote us a check.

We talked about buying another boat but ended up using the money to pay off some of my helicopter ride and medical bills. We did rent a houseboat on Smith Mountain Lake for a few days before summer ended though.

We got stuck on a sandbar and Holly broke her left ankle when she missed the bottom rung of a ladder. She had to wear a big boot and milked the injury for months.

Also, I found out recently that it's bad luck to have bananas onboard a boat and, while we were cleaning and prepping Bushpig for the lake, Holly ate a banana. I'm not saying the fire and the boat sinking was entirely her fault but it's worth noting.

Free 2D Glasses
Experience the world in stunning 2D. Simply cut out and glue flaps.

GLUE

GLUE

About the Author

To understand David Thorne, you have to ignore the fact that he's pretty. What you see is cosmetic glamour, fresh wax on a Formula 1, an attractive sheen that belies the power and deeper sense of purpose underneath.

The impoverished people of Jaramillo in Baja California, for instance, wouldn't recognize this David Thorne. They might remember a blonde dynamo with dirty fingernails who gave up an entire summer break to build them a schoolhouse a couple of years ago, but this glossy gringo is a stranger. Poised, straightforward and razor-sharp, Thorne hates labels but "adventurer" would not be far off the mark. Consider his first job as a flight attendant on a hot-air balloon, casually serving champagne to joy riders high above the California desert.

"I'm not afraid of doing most of the things others are afraid of doing," he tells us. "I'd rather do something physically dangerous than go along on an even keel."

That's an apt metaphor because David is a sailor. More than that, at 39, he's a sea creature, at home on or in the water. He has made a pact with the ocean that weekend tars and motorboat dilettantes only dream about.

"I like being on the ocean away from people; you wake up and look out and there's nothing around you but water. You could be on your way to China if your navigation is off. Sailing is sensuous. I love the smell of the water, the feeling of the wind and the sun. If there's a storm, it's even more exciting. You know the boat could capsize at any moment. Or fog. I've been in fog so thick at night you couldn't see the bow from the stern. Once I heard a horn blast in the fog. It was one of those big boats with containers on them."

Indeed, the only thing David cares as much about as sailing is learning. He virtually conquered his level 3 NVQ diploma in hairdressing and his current college course will lead him to a certification in psychocosmetology - the study of the relationship between being positive and looking great.

"It's a fairly new field that I find especially fascinating," he says. In typical Thorne fashion, he's low-key about his considerable intelligence. "I think it's harder to be dumb than to be smart," he laughs, brushing a golden strand of hair from his eyes, "I mean, it takes a lot of effort."

Following a brief stint as a magician's assistant in Pierre, North Dakota, David decided to pursue his education in the palm-shaded halls of the Hawaii Institute of Hair Design. There are two ways to get to Hawaii; David opted for the more difficult.

With a smile on his face and the wind in his hair, he sailed a 44-foot sloop out of Newport Beach and across the big pond.

Two weeks on the Pacific is certainly no Sunday sail. On a well-equipped boat with an experienced crew, the odds of making Waikiki harbor change minute to minute with the whims of the sea. At best, it could be boring; at worst, fatal. With perfect weather all the way, David made it in 16 days.

David currently spends a lot of time with his nose in books but we don't think it'll be long before he strikes out on another fantastic adventure. Like a modern day Robert Frost, he told us: "I'd rather hike across a muddy paddock than follow a path with arrows."

Books by the Same Author
Walk It Off, Princess
ISBN 978-0-9886895-8-9

The sixth release by bestselling author David Thorne featuring all new essays and emails including: The Spot, Signs, Cantilevers and many more.

"I once stabbed a stripper in the car park of Paradise City Gentlemen's Club. Her body is buried in a field at coordinates 38°51'40.1N 78°51'41.2W."

JM, Senior Citizen

Books by the Same Author

The Internet is a Playground

ISBN 978-1585428816

Features over 200 pages of emails and articles from 27bslash6, plus over 160 pages of new material. Debuting at #4 on *The New York Times* Best Seller list, *The Internet is a Playground* is the first release by David Thorne. It makes a nice present, protects against tigers, and can be read while hiding in small places.

"There is usually a fine line between genius and insanity, but in this case it has become very blurred. Some of the funniest and most clever writing I have read in years."

WIRED Magazine

Books by the Same Author
I'll Go Home Then;
It's Warm and Has Chairs

ISBN 978-0-9886895-3-4

More emails, more articles, more exclusive content. *I'll Go Home Then; It's Warm and Has Chairs* is the second bestselling release by author David Thorne.

"Simultaneously stupid and brilliant. An astonishingly funny second book by the author of *The Internet is a Playground*."

The Huffington Post

Books by the Same Author

Look Evelyn, Duck Dynasty Wiper Blades. We should Get Them

ISBN 978-0-9886895-2-7

Featuring all new, never before published material, *Look Evelyn, Duck Dynasty Wiper Blades. We Should Get Them* is the bestselling third release by author David Thorne.

"Instantly engaging and very funny. Those new to Thorne's unique brand of humour are in for a real treat."

Good Reads

Books by the Same Author
That's Not How You Wash a Squirrel
ISBN 978-0-9886895-9-6

That's Not How You Wash a Squirrel is the fourth release by *New York Times* bestselling author David Thorne and features over two hundred pages of brand new, never before seen essays and emails including: Ride of the Valkyries, Squirrel, Deer Camp, Tomotes, Gypsies, Cloud Backgrounds and many more.

"Clever and funny. Packed with stories and correspondences that will leave you chuckling long after you have finished them."

The Washington Post

Books by the Same Author
Wrap It In a Bit of Cheese Like You're Tricking the Dog
ISBN 978-0-9886895-5-8

The fifth release by *New York Times* bestselling author David Thorne featuring over two hundred pages of brand new, never before seen essays and emails including: Production Meeting, Robert the Telemarketing Raccoon, Mrs Gillespie, Smiling & Nodding, Ughhh, Raymond, and many more. Foreword by Patti Ford *Insane In The Mom Brain*

"Clever, awkward and laugh-out-loud funny."

The Huffington Post

Also Available

David Thorne Hums the Theme from Space 1999

And Other Christmas Classics

ASIN B01FRFSTOQ / 60 minute CD

Forged almost entirely from thermoplastic polymers, this CD contains over 26 popular Christmas tracks including the theme from that movie about the big boat and that other one about the two guys.

"You need to get a life. I listened to about 1 second of it and threw it in the bin. Don't send me your stupid shit and I expect the stuff about me on the website to be deleted. I spoke to a lawyer and he said I could sue you for defamation."

Lucius Thaller

Also Available
The Collected Works *of* 27b/6 Victorian Edition
ISBN 978-0-9886895-1-0

All the 27b/6 articles in one volume - illustrated and abridged for polite society. Sure to be a hit at your next local council meeting or church fundraiser, *The Collected Works of 27b/6 ~ Victorian Edition* will take pride of place on your bookshelf next to the dictionary you don't remember buying and the rock that might be a meteorite. Free sticker with signed copies.

"So it's stories from your books and website edited down to a paragraph each? That's kind of stupid."

Holly Thorne

Printed in Great Britain
by Amazon